CQR Pocket Guide
Writing: Grammar, Usage, and Style

Parts of Speech

Noun: Names a person, place, or thing—either abstract (*Love* is wonderful.) or concrete (The *flower* bloomed.)

Verb: Expresses action (He *jumped*.) or state of being (She *will be* late.)

Pronoun: Replaces a noun or pronoun (Tom found *his* watch.)

Adjective: Describes or limits nouns or pronouns (She is a *pretty* girl.)

Adverb: Describes or limits verbs, adjectives, and other adverbs (He runs *quickly*.)

Preposition: Shows relationships between a noun or pronoun and another noun or pronoun (The towel was *on* the floor.)

Conjunction: Links words, phrases, or clauses (Mary *and* I went home.)

Tips For Using Parts of Speech

- Capitalize proper nouns: My uncle was in Desert Storm.
- Make nouns plural by adding *-s* or *-es* in most cases: The bears awoke.
- Make nouns possessive by adding *-'s* to singular nouns (dog's bone) or the apostrophe alone if the noun is plural (Smiths' home).
- Singular nouns require singular verbs: My sister laughs often.
- Plural nouns require plural verbs: My sisters laugh often.
- Collective nouns are considered singular: The Congress is in session.
- A verb tense indicates the action of the verb.

Six Most Common Verb Tenses

Present	*(I walk)*	Present Perfect *(I have walked)*
Past	*(I walked)*	Past Perfect *(I had walked)*
Future	*(I will walk)*	Future Perfect *(I will have walked)*

Tips for Writing Good Sentences

- Fix **run-on sentences** by rewriting the sentence or adding punctuation between two independent clauses.
- Correct **sentence fragments** by adding the missing subject or predicate to phrases or subordinate clauses.
- Eliminate **faulty agreement** by making subjects and predicates agree in person and number.
- Combine short, choppy sentences for a **smooth style**.

CQR Pocket Guide
Writing: Grammar, Usage, and Style

Sentence Review

Phrases are groups of related words missing either a subject or a predicate.

Clauses are groups of related words with a subject or predicate that are part of a longer sentence.

Sentences express a complete thought using a subject and predicate.

Tips for Better Punctuation

- **Commas** should be used to join introductory clauses, after introductory clauses and phrases, to set off interrupting elements, with restrictive and nonrestrictive elements, with appositives, and between items or modifiers in a series.
- **Semicolons** are used to join closely connected independent clauses and between items in a series.
- **Colons** are used to introduce a list, formal statement, or restatement in a sentence.
- **Punctuation** usually belongs inside quotation marks.

Tips for Word Usage

- Watch out for frequently confused words.
- Hyphenate most compound adjectives that appear before a noun.
- Generally, spell compound adjectives that follow a noun and words with prefixes or suffixes as one word.
- Most compound adverbs are spelled as two words.
- Eliminate clichés, jargon, faddish words, and slang in your writing.
- Avoid redundant expressions and wordiness in writing.

The Writing Process

Prewriting	Rewriting	Writing
Evaluate the audience	Research	Compose a working thesis
Consider the assignment	Develop main ideas	Outline
Choose a topic	Organize ideas	Write first draft
	Revise	
	Edit	Write final draft

CliffsQuickReview™ Writing: Grammar, Usage, and Style

By Jean Eggenschwiler, M.A.
and Emily Dotson Biggs

WILEY

Wiley Publishing, Inc.

About the Authors

Jean Eggenschwiler, MA is a graduate of U. C. Berkeley and Stanford University. She has taught English and Composition in high school and worked as a business editor and writer.

Emily Dotson Biggs is a graduate of the University of North Carolina and Murray State University. She is currently an adjunct instructor at Paducah Community College and Murray State University and has taught English to students from kindergarten to college.

Publisher's Acknowledgments

Editorial

Project Editor: Howard Gelman

Acquisitions Editor: Sherry Gomoll

Copy Editor: Howard Gelman

Editorial Administrator: Michelle Hacker

Production

Indexer: TECHBOOKS Production Services

Proofreader: TECHBOOKS Production Services

Wiley Indianapolis Composition Services

CliffsQuickReview™ *Writing: Grammar, Usage, and Style*

Published by:

Wiley Publishing, Inc.

909 Third Avenue

New York, NY 10022

www.wiley.com

Copyright © 2001 Wiley Publishing, Inc., New York, New York

Library of Congress Control Number: 2001024142

ISBN: 0-7645-6393-9

Printed in the United States of America

20 19 18 17 16 15 14 13

1O/RV/QW/QT/IN

Published by Wiley Publishing, Inc., New York, NY

Published simultaneously in Canada

Table of Contents

Introduction

Effective writing is an essential communication skill that is necessary in personal relationships and in almost every profession. Fortunately, writing is a skill you can learn! Whether you are a high school or college student, a business writer, or just someone interested in improving your written communication, this book will help you become a better writer. It is organized to be useful to both the beginner and experienced writer.

This book provides an easy to follow, practical guide to the fundamentals of writing, including information about grammar, sentences, punctuation, words, and the writing process. First, you review the basic rules of grammar, including the parts of speech and their usage. Next, you see how phrases, clauses and sentences are constructed, and you are given tips on avoiding some of the basic errors in constructing sentences. Then, you discover how to take the mystery out of punctuation rules, including frustrating comma decisions. After this, you explore word choice and usage and find some helpful suggestions for avoiding common problems that can occur when choosing words. Finally, in a simple step-by-step guide, you learn how to go through the process that leads to good writing.

Why You Need This Book

Can you answer yes to any of these questions?

- Do you need to review the fundamentals of grammar?
- Do you want to know how to write better?
- Do you want to effectively communicate your ideas in writing?
- Do you want to be able to understand and evaluate writing?
- Do you need a course supplement to English?
- Do you need to prepare for any test that evaluates writing skills?
- Do you need a concise, comprehensive reference for grammar and writing?
- Is effective writing important in your job or personal life?

If so, then CliffsQuickReview *Writing: Grammar, Usage, and Style* is for you!

How to Use This Book

You can use this book in any way that fits your personal style for study and review—you decide what works best with your needs. You can either read the book from cover to cover, or just look for the information you want, and put it back on the shelf for later. Here are just a few ways you can search for topics:

- Review the Pocket Guide for a brief highlight of the essential concepts.

- Look for areas of interest in the book's Table of Contents, or use the index to find specific topics.

- Read the book looking for your topic in the running heads.

- Look in the glossary for all the important terms and definitions.

- Get a glimpse of what you'll gain from a chapter by reading through the "Chapter Check-In" at the beginning of each chapter.

- Test your knowledge in the Chapter Checkout quizzes or CQR Review.

- Discover additional information in the Resource Center.

- Skim the book for special terms in bold type.

- Flip through the book until you find what you're looking for—we organized the book in a logical, task-oriented way.

Visit Our Web Site

A great resource, `www.cliffsnotes.com`, features review materials, valuable Internet links, quizzes, and more to enhance your learning. The site also features timely articles and tips, plus downloadable versions of many CliffsNotes books.

When you stop by our site, don't hesitate to share your thoughts about this book or any Wiley product. Just click the Talk to Us button. We welcome your feedback!

Chapter 1
NOUNS

Chapter Check-In

❑ Identifying proper nouns and gerunds

❑ Using collective nouns to identify groups

❑ Understanding singular and plural nouns

❑ Using possessive nouns to show ownership

❑ Making nouns and verbs agree

A noun is a part of speech that names a person, place, or thing. Many different kinds of nouns are used in the English language. Some are specific for people, places, or events, and some represent groups or collections. Some nouns aren't even nouns; they're verbs acting like nouns in sentences.

Nouns can be singular, referring to one thing, or plural, referring to more than one thing. Nouns can be possessive as well; possessive nouns indicate ownership or a close relationship. Regardless of the type, nouns should always agree with their verbs in sentences; use singular verbs with singular nouns and plural verbs with plural nouns. You have to know how a noun works in order to write an effective sentence.

Proper Nouns

If a noun names a specific person or place, or a particular event or group, it is called a **proper noun** and is always capitalized. Some examples are *Eleanor Roosevelt, Niagara Falls, Dracula, the Federal Bureau of Investigation, the Great Depression, and Desert Storm.* This seems simple enough.

Unfortunately, some writers assign proper-noun status fairly indiscriminately to other words, sprinkling capital letters freely throughout their prose. For example, the *Manhattan Project* is appropriately capitalized because it is a historic project, the name given to the specific wartime effort to design and build the first nuclear weapons. But *project* should not be capitalized when referring to a club's project to clean up the campus. Similarly, the *Great Depression* should be capitalized because it refers to the specific historical period of economic failure that began with the stock market collapse in 1929. When the word *depression* refers to other economic hard times, however, it is not a proper noun but a common noun and should not be capitalized. Some flexibility in capitalizing nouns is acceptable. A writer may have a valid reason for capitalizing a particular term, for example, and some companies use style guides that dictate capital letters for job titles such as manager. But often the use of a capital outside the basic rule is an effort to give a word an air of importance, and you should avoid it.

Verbs Used as Nouns

One special case is when a verb is used as a noun. Here the verb form is altered and it serves the same function as a noun in the sentence. This type of noun is called a **gerund**.

The gerund

A noun created from the *-ing* form of a verb is called a gerund. Like other nouns, gerunds act as subjects and objects in sentences.

> *Sleeping* sometimes serves as an escape from *studying*.

The gerunds *sleeping* and *studying* are *-ing* forms of the verbs *sleep* and *study*. *Sleeping* is the noun functioning as the subject of this sentence, and *studying* is an object (in this case, the object of a preposition—see Chapter 5).

The problem gerund

Gerunds can sometimes be difficult to use properly in a sentence. What problems will you have with gerunds?

- When a noun or pronoun precedes a gerund, use the possessive case of the noun or pronoun. (For the possessive case of the pronoun, see Chapter 3).

    > *Jane's sleeping* was sometimes an escape from studying.

- Even when you think that the word before the gerund looks like an object, use the possessive case.

    > Jane was annoyed by *Bill's studying*.

    NOT   Jane was annoyed by *Bill studying*.

Collective Nouns

A word that stands for a group of things is called a **collective noun.** In fact, the word *group* itself is a collective noun. Here are a few others: *club, team, committee, furniture, jury, Congress, swarm, herd.*

Usually these nouns are treated as singular, since the emphasis is on a unit rather than its parts.

> The *team is* going on the bus.
>
> The *committee wants* to find a solution to the problem.

But when you want to emphasize the individual parts of a group, you may treat a collective noun as plural.

> The *team have* argued about going on the bus.
>
> The *committee want* different solutions to the problem.

If the plural sounds awkward, try rewriting.

> The *team members have* argued about going on the bus.
>
> *Committee members disagree* about solutions to the problem.

Singular and Plural Nouns

The term **number** refers to whether a noun is singular or plural. Most nouns can be either, depending on whether you are talking about one thing *(dog)* or more than one *(dogs).* You know the basic rule of adding *-s* to make the plural of a noun, and you also know that many nouns don't follow that rule—for example, *sheep* (singular), *sheep* (plural); *enemy, enemies; wharf, wharves, hero, heroes, goose, geese,* and so on. You should check your dictionary if you're not sure about a plural. Do not add *-'s* to a singular form to make it plural, even if the noun you are using is a family name: *the Taylors,* not *the Taylor's; donkeys,* not *donkey's; taxis,* not *taxi's.*

The singular and plural forms of some nouns with Latin and Greek endings can cause trouble. The noun *data,* for example, is actually a plural; *datum* is the singular.

> The final *datum* is not consistent with the preceding *data,* which *are* positive.

Although today the plural *data* is widely treated as singular, keep the distinction, particularly in scientific writing.

Here are some other examples of Latin and Greek singular and plural words: *bacterium, bacteria, criterion, criteria, medium, media; alumnus* (masculine singular)/*alumni* (masculine plural), *alumna* (feminine singular)/*alumnae* (feminine plural). If you are writing about television, use *medium*. If you are writing about radio, television, and the press, use *media*.

Possessive Case of Nouns

The **possessive case** of a noun is used to show ownership (*Allan's car, my sister's house*) or another close relationship (*the chairman's friends, the cup's handle, the university's position*).

Problems with possessives

What causes problems with possessive nouns is uncertainty: Do I add an -*'s* or just an apostrophe? Follow this rule: for singular nouns, add 's, even if the noun ends in an -*s* or -*z* sound: *dog's, house's, Wes's, Keats's*. But make an exception when an added -*s* would lead to three closely bunched *s* or *z* sounds (*Jesus', Ulysses'*) or in names of more than one syllable with an unaccented ending pronounced -*eez* (*Empedocles', Socrates', Euripides'*). Greek names often fall into this category.

For most plural possessive nouns, add an apostrophe alone: *several months' bills, many Rumanians' apartments, the encyclopedias' differences, the Rolling Stones' travel plans*. If a plural noun doesn't end in -*s*, add -*'s*, just as you would with a singular noun: *women's issues, mice's tails*.

Switching to an *of* construction

When a possessive noun sounds awkward, use an *of* construction instead. This is a safe and often preferable way to indicate the relationship: *the top of the page* instead of *the page's top; the lawn of the building on the corner* instead of *the building on the corner's lawn, the main characters of Pride and Prejudice* instead of *Pride and Prejudice's main characters; the novels of Dickens* instead of *Dickens's novels*.

Joint ownership

One last word about possessive nouns: When you are indicating joint ownership, give the possessive form to the final name only, such as *Abbott and Costello's movies; Tom and Dawn's dinner party; Smith, Wilson, and Nelson's partnership*.

Agreement of Nouns and Verbs

Agreement is an important concept in grammar and a source of many writing errors. It will come up again under pronouns (Chapter 3) and under sentence construction (Chapter 7).

Verbs must agree with their nouns, which means that a singular noun requires a singular verb, and a plural noun requires a plural verb.

> The *dog jumps* up and down. (singular)
> The *dogs jump* up and down. (plural)

Remember that a noun ending in *-s* is often a plural, whereas a verb ending in *-s* is usually singular: *runs* in my pantyhose (plural noun); he *runs* (singular verb).

Nouns with Latin or Greek endings and nouns that look plural but sometimes take singular verbs can cause agreement problems.

> The *data indicate* that the test samples are more affected by heat than the control group samples.

Since *data* is the plural form of *datum,* use the plural form of the verb (in this case, *indicate).* In the following example, *criteria* is plural. Use the plural form of the verb *(are).*

> The *criteria* for judging an entry *are* listed in the brochure.

Rights, which is a plural form, is treated as singular in the following example because *human rights* is a unit, an issue of concern.

> *Human rights is* an issue that affects everyone.

If you wanted to emphasize the rights individually, you could use the plural verb:

> *Human rights are* ignored in many countries.

In the next example, *miles* is the plural form, but *fifty miles* is used here to name a unit of distance and therefore takes a singular verb:

> *Fifty miles is* not such a long distance.

Statistics looks plural, and in many situations would be treated as plural, for example,

> *Statistics is* the subject I most want to avoid.
> *Statistics are* being gathered to show that women are better drivers than men.

In the first example, *statistics* refers to a subject of study, so the singular is appropriate.

Among other frequently used nouns that can take either a singular or plural verb, depending on whether the emphasis is on a single unit or individual items, are *number, majority,* and *minority.*

> The *number* of people coming *is* surprising.
>
> A *number* of people *are* coming.
>
> A *number* like five thousand *is* what he had in mind.

With *number,* use this rule. If it is preceded by *the,* always use the singular. If it is preceded by *a,* use the singular or plural, depending on whether you are thinking of a single unit or individual items.

With *majority* and *minority*, the key is to decide whether you want to emphasize individual people or things or whether you want to emphasize the single unit.

> The *majority is* opposed to the measure. (singular = single unit)
>
> A *minority* of the younger people *refuse* to concede the point. (plural = individuals)

Chapter Checkout

Q&A

1. Identify the underlined nouns in the following sentences as common or proper nouns.

   a. Dylan plans to go to <u>college</u> in the fall.
   b. Mary Lagan was accepted to <u>Watson College</u>.

2. Identify the underlined nouns in the following sentences as a collective noun, singular noun, or a gerund.

   a. The <u>commission</u> plans to review the report.
   b. <u>Running</u> is fun.
   c. My <u>coach</u> is great.
   d. The <u>firm</u> established a strict dress code

3. Match the underlined nouns with their correct definition.

   a. My <u>dog's</u> bone was lost.   singular
   b. The <u>women</u> meet for lunch.   singular possessive
   c. My <u>sons'</u> cars need to be washed.   plural
   d. A <u>girl</u> lost her scarf on the bus.   plural possessive

4. Fill in the blank with the correct form of the verb to make the noun and verb agree in the following sentences.

  a. Margaret and Tommy _____ happy. (look, looks)
  b. Neither Patrick nor Alex _____ the answer. (know, knows)
  c. John, as well as Ali and Griffin, _____ to visit Orlando. (plan, plans)
  d. Many of the causes of global warming _____ unknown to scientists. (are, is)
  e. The danger of diving _____ not discourage Lily. (do, does)
  f. While wearing her school uniform, Tessie _____ for charity. (dance, dances)

Answers: 1. a. common b. proper 2. a. collective b. gerund c. singular d. collective 3. a. singular possessive b. plural c. plural possessive d. singular 4. a. look b. knows c. plans d. are e. does f. dances.

Chapter 2
VERBS

A verb is a part of speech that expresses action or state of being or connects a subject to a complement. They indicate whether the subject performs an action, called active voice, or receives the action, called passive voice. Verbs can be transitive or intransitive. Verb tenses are formed according to person, number, and tense.

Verbs also have moods, which are classifications that indicate the attitude of the speaker. Problems with verbs are often the result of an incorrect tense, or the difficulty many writers have with the past and past participle forms of irregular verbs. Verbs play a key role in constructing sentences.

Action Verbs

An **action verb** animates a sentence, either physically (*swim, jump, drop, whistle*) or mentally (*think, dream, believe, suppose, love*). Verbs make sentences move, sometimes dramatically, sometimes quietly.

> She *leaped* high into the air, *twirled*, *landed* on the floor, and *ran* from the room.
> He *thought* of her beauty, *imagined* her smile, *yearned* for her presence.

Linking Verbs

Some verbs don't express action but help complete statements about the subject by describing or identifying it. These verbs are called **linking verbs.**

>Diane *is* happy.
>
>Clement *feels* hot.
>
>Maria *is* a doctor.
>
>The music *sounds* good.

The sentences don't tell you what Diane, Clement, Maria, and the music *did* but rather what they *are*. Linking verbs "link" their subjects to a classification, state of being, or quality. In the sentences above, *happy, hot, doctor,* and *good* are called **complements** of the linking verbs (see Chapter 3). Table 2-1 lists common linking verbs.

Table 2-1   Common Linking Verbs

appear	grow	smell
be	look	sound
become	remain	taste
feel	seem	

Some of these verbs can be both linking and action verbs.

>Clement *felt* hot. (linking verb)
>
>Clement *felt* along the wall for the light switch. (action verb)
>
>The dog *smelled* bad. (linking verb)
>
>The dog *smelled* the man's boots. (action verb)

A quick way to tell whether a verb is functioning as a linking verb is to see whether you can replace it with a form of the verb *to be* and still have a reasonable sentence. For example, test the two sentences above by replacing *smelled* with *was*.

>The dog *was* bad. (yes)
>
>The dog *was* the man's boots. (no)

Linking verbs operate differently than action verbs. First, while action verbs are modified by adverbs, linking verbs are followed by adjectives.

>This cheese *smells strong.*
>
>NOT This cheese *smells strongly.*

This rule is discussed in Chapter 4.

Also, a pronoun following the linking verb *to be* should be in the subjective case rather than the objective case.

> It *was she*.
>
> NOT It *was her*.

This rule is discussed in Chapter 3.

Active and Passive Voice

The term **voice** refers to the form of a verb indicating whether the subject performs an action (**active voice**) or receives the action (**passive voice**).

> Mary *smashed* the ball over the net. (active voice)
>
> The ball *was smashed* over the net by Mary. (passive voice)

Use the active voice whenever you can; it conveys more energy than the passive voice and also results in more concise writing. (See Chapter 13.)

Use the passive voice, however, when you don't know the actor, when you don't want to name the actor, or when you want to emphasize the person or thing acted upon rather than the actor. The passive voice is often appropriate in scientific writing.

> When we returned, the *car had been towed*.
>
> I regret that a *mistake was made*.
>
> *Gold was discovered* there early in the last century.
>
> His *mother was rushed* to the hospital by the police.
>
> A *change* in structure *was found* in the experimental group.

Transitive and Intransitive Verbs

A transitive verb, used with a direct object, transmits action to an object and may also have an indirect object, which indicates to or for whom the action is done. In contrast, an intransitive verb never takes an object.

Transitive verbs

A **transitive verb** takes a **direct object;** that is, the verb transmits action to an object.

> He *sent* the *letter.* (*letter* = direct object of *sent*)
>
> She *gave* the *lecture.* (*lecture* = direct object of *gave*)

In these sentences, something is being done to an object.

A transitive verb can also have an **indirect object** that precedes the direct object. The indirect object tells to or for whom the action is done, although the words *to* and *for* are not used. In the following examples, notice the difference between the direct and indirect objects.

The direct object *(letter)* receives the action *(sent)*. The indirect object *(Robert)* is the person to whom the letter is sent.

> He *sent Robert* the *letter.*

The direct object *(lecture)* receives the action *(gave)*. The indirect object *(class)* is the group to whom the lecture is given.

> She *gave* her *class* the lecture.

Learn to recognize words that are direct and indirect objects of verbs. When these words are pronouns, they must be in the objective case. See Chapter 3 for an explanation of pronoun cases.

Intransitive verbs

An **intransitive** verb does not take an object.

> She *sleeps* too much.

> He *complains* frequently.

In these sentences, nothing receives the action of the verbs *sleep* and *complain.*

Many verbs can be either transitive or intransitive.

> She *sings* every day. (no object = intransitive)

> She *sings spirituals.* (*spirituals* receives the action of *sings* = transitive)

Verbals: Gerunds, Infinitives, and Participles

In one sense, the three verbals—**gerunds, infinitives, and participles**—should not be covered in this section on verbs. Although formed from verbs, verbals are never used alone as the action words in sentences; instead, they function as nouns, adjectives, or adverbs. These verbals are important in phrases (discussed in Chapter 6).

- The gerund (see Chapter 1) ends in *-ing* and functions as a noun.

  Jumping is fun.

  He liked *skiing.*

- The infinitive is the base form of a verb with *to.* Usually it also functions as a noun, although it can be an adjective or adverb.

  To jump is fun. (noun; subject of *is*)

  I like *to ski.* (noun; object of *like)*

  She had a suggestion *to offer.*(adjective modifying *suggestion*)

  He called *to warn* her. (adverb modifying *called*)

- A participle is a verb that ends in *-ing* (present participle) or *-ed, -d, -t, -en, -n* (past participle). Participles may function as adjectives, describing or modifying nouns.

  The *dancing* bear entertained the crowd.

  The *beaten* man hobbled into the woods.

- But participles have another function. Used with helping verbs such as *to be* and *to have,* they form several verb **tenses.**

  She *is thinking* of the children.

  The boat *had been cleaned* before they arrived.

Forming Verb Tenses

To write correctly, you need to know both how to form verb tenses and when to use them. Verb tenses are formed according to person, number, and tense. They are the key to coherent sentence structure.

Tense, person, and number

Person refers to the subject or object of the verb. Number identifies whether a verb is singular or plural. A few terms will help you to understand how verb tenses are formed.

- **Tense:** refers to time; when is the action (or state of being) of the verb taking place?

- **Person:** refers to the person (or thing) that is a subject or object.

  First person: *I, we* go; she spoke to *me, us*

Second person: *you, you* (all) go; she spoke to *you, you* (all)

Third person: *he, she, it* goes, *they* go; she spoke *to him, her, it, them*

■ **Number:** simply refers to whether a verb is singular *(he goes)* or plural *(they go)*

In the sentence *The horse runs in the pasture, runs* is the third-person singular of the present tense of the verb *run.*

The six tenses

Although there are more, six tenses are commonly used in English.

■ **Present:** action going on now

■ **Past:** action that is over

■ **Future:** action that has yet to take place

■ **Present perfect:** action in past time in relation to present time

■ **Past perfect:** action in past time in relation to another past time

■ **Future perfect:** action in a future time in relation to another time farther in the future

Definitions of the perfect tenses are difficult to understand without examples. Tables 2-2, 2-3, 2-4, 2-5, 2-6, and 2-7 show the regular verb *to walk* and the irregular verb *to be* in the six tenses. Regular verbs, like *to walk*, form the past tense and the perfect tenses by adding *-d* or *-ed* to the present tense. But like *to be*, many English verbs are irregular, forming their past tenses in various ways. A list of frequently used irregular verbs is provided at the end of the chapter.

Table 2-2   Present Tense

	Singular	*Plural*
First Person	*I walk*	*we walk*
	I am	*we are*
Second Person	*you walk*	*you walk*
	you are	*you are*
Third Person	*he, she, it walks*	*they walk*
	he, she, it is	*they are*

Table 2-3   Past Tense

	Singular	*Plural*
First Person	*I walked*	*we walked*
	I was	*we were*
Second Person	*you walked*	*you walked*
	you were	*you were*
Third Person	*he, she, it walked*	*they walked*
	he, she, it was	*they were*

Table 2-4   Future Tense

	Singular	*Plural*
First Person	*I will walk*	*we will walk*
	I will be	*we will be*
Second Person	*you will walk*	*you will walk*
	you will be	*you will be*
Third Person	*he, she, it will walk*	*they will walk*
	he, she, it will be	*they will be*

Note that in the future tense, traditionally *shall* has been used for *will* in the first-person singular and plural: I *shall* walk, we *shall* walk. In modem usage, however, *will* has replaced *shall* almost entirely. Although either is correct, *shall* produces an unusually formal effect.

Table 2-5   Present Perfect Tense

	Singular	*Plural*
First Person	*I have walked*	*we have walked*
	I have been	*we have been*
Second Person	*you have walked*	*you have walked*
	you have been	*you have been*
Third Person	*he, she, it has walked*	*they have walked*
	he, she, it has been	*they have been*

Table 2-6   Past Perfect Tense

	Singular	*Plural*
First Person	*I had walked*	*we had walked*
	I had been	*we had been*
Second Person	*you had walked*	*you had walked*
	you had been	*you had been*
Third Person	*he, she, it had walked*	*they had walked*
	he, she, it had been	*they had been*

Table 2-7   Future Perfect Tense

	Singular	*Plural*
First Person	*I will have walked*	*we will have walked*
	I will have been	*we will have been*
Second Person	*you will have walked*	*you will have walked*
	you will have been	*you will have been*
Third Person	*he, she, it will have walked*	*they will have walked*
	he, she, it will have been	*they will have been*

Using the Tenses

Tense indicates when the action or state of being occurs, and knowing how to use it helps convey your meaning. Forming tenses can be simple or complicated.

Present, past, and future

The present, past, and future tenses are part of our everyday language and as writers we are able to use these forms with ease. The present tense indicates action occurring now.

He *calls* her on the phone.

Sometimes, the present tense can also be used to indicate future action.

Her plane *arrives* on Friday.

The past tense indicates action completed in the past.

He *called* her on the phone.

The future tense is used for action that will occur at a future time.

He *will call* her on the phone.

Present perfect

The present perfect tense, formed with *has* or *have* and the past participle of the verb, indicates action that occurred in the past and has continued into the present.

I *have called* you for a year. (And I am still calling you.)

This contrasts with the simple past tense, which suggests an action that both began and ended in the past.

I *called* you for a year. (But I am no longer calling you.)

The present perfect tense can also be used when you want to emphasize an action that occurred in the past but at no definite time.

I *have called* many times.

Past perfect

The past perfect tense, formed with *had* and the past participle of the verb, indicates an action completed in the past *before* another action completed in the past.

After I *had called* you ten times, I *asked* the operator to check your number.

Had called is a past action that was completed *before* asking the operator, another completed past action.

In the following example, his being sober for a year *preceded* the accident: past before past.

He *had been sober* for a year when the accident happened.

Future perfect

The future perfect tense, formed with *will have* and the past participle of the verb, is used for action that will be completed in the future *before* another future action.

By next week, I *will have called* you more than a hundred times.

Calling more than a hundred times will take place *before* next week. In the following example, his achieving sobriety for a year will *precede* the future arrival of his daughter.

He *will have been* sober for a year by the time his daughter arrives.

Moods of the Verb

Verb moods are classifications that indicate the attitude of the speaker. Verbs have three moods—the indicative, the imperative, and the subjunctive.

The indicative and imperative

The indicative and the imperative moods are easy to understand. You use the **indicative** mood in most statements and questions.

He *walks* every day after lunch.

Does he *believe* in the good effects of exercise?

You use the **imperative** in requests and commands. Imperative statements have an understood subject of you and therefore take second-person verbs.

Sit down. ([*You*] sit down.)

Please *take* a number. ([*You*] please take a number.)

The subjunctive

The tenses of the **subjunctive** mood are formed differently from the indicative tenses, and the subjunctive is used in special kinds of statements. Today, the most common use of the subjunctive mood is in contrary-to-fact or hypothetical statements. In your own writing, you must decide which statements should be in the subjunctive. If something is likely to happen, use the indicative. If something is purely hypothetical, or contrary to fact, use the subjunctive.

■ **Present tense subjunctive**

If I *were* king, you would be queen. (In the subjunctive, *were* is used for all persons.)

If he *worked,* he could earn high wages.

■ **Past tense subjunctive**

If I *had been* king, you would have been queen.

If he *had worked,* he could have earned high wages.

These contrary-to-fact statements have two clauses: the *if* clause and the consequences clause. The forms of the verbs in these clauses are different from those of verbs used in the indicative mood.

In the *if* clause, use the subjunctive. Table 2-8 shows how it is formed.

Table 2-8   Present subjunctive

Verb *to be: were*	*If I were king, If he were king.*
Other verbs*: worked*	*If I worked, If he worked.*

Note that the subjunctive present tense is the same as the indicative past tense.

Table 2-9   Past subjunctive

Verb *to be: had been*	*If I had been king, If he had been king.*
Other verbs: *had worked*	*If I had worked, If he had worked.*

Note in Table 2-9 how the subjunctive past tense is the same as the indicative past perfect tense.

In the **consequences clause**, use the conditional (Table 2-10 and 2-11), which is formed with *could* or *would*.

Table 2-10   Present conditional

could, would + base form of verb	*You would be queen; He could earn high wages.*

Table 2-11   Past conditional

could, would + have	*You would have been queen;*
+ past participle of verb	*He could have earned high wages.*

Not all clauses beginning with *if* are contrary to fact. When an *if* clause indicates something that is likely to happen, use the indicative not the subjunctive.

> If I *study* hard, I *will pass* the test.
> If his fever *continues* to fall, he *will recover.*

Problems with Verbs

Writers sometimes use an incorrect tense or don't know how to use the past participle forms of irregular verbs. Using verb tenses imprecisely or inconsistently can also irritate a reader.

Illogical time sequence

Recognize time sequences in your writing and choose verb tenses that logically reflect that sequence. Sometimes the choice of a tense clearly affects your meaning.

> Esther *worked* at the department store for a year.

Use the past tense to indicate a completed action. Esther no longer works at the department store.

> Esther *has worked* at the department store for a year.

Use the present perfect tense to indicate that a past action is continuing in the present. Esther still works at the department store.

> Esther *had worked* at the department store for a year.

Use the past perfect tense to indicate that something else happened after Esther's year. For example, Esther *had worked* at the department store for a year when she was asked to take over sporting goods.

When to use the perfect tense

Learn to use the perfect tenses when they are appropriate to your meaning. Don't limit yourself to the simple past tense when writing about past action. In the following sentences, for example, a perfect tense should have been used to establish time sequence.

> The car wash *stood* where the library *was*. (no)
> All the things you *told* me I *heard* before. (no)

In the first sentence, since the library was in the location before the car wash—it would be difficult for them to occupy the same space at the same time—past perfect should be used for the second verb.

> The car wash *stood* where the library *had been*.

The logic of the second sentence dictates that *heard* should be in the past perfect tense. The word *before* is an obvious clue that the hearing took place before the telling, even though both actions were completed in the past.

> All the things you *told* me, I *had heard* before.

Faulty *if* clauses

The past perfect tense should also be used in a subjunctive past tense "*if* clause".

> If she *had thought* of it, she would have called you.

A common error is to use the conditional *would have* or *could have* in both clauses. *Would have* and *could have* should be used only in the clause that states the consequences.

> If I *had wanted* to, I *would have* made cookies.
>
> NOT   If I *would have wanted* to, I *would have* made cookies.

> If we *had brought* matches, we *could have* made a bonfire.
>
> NOT   If we *would have brought* matches, we *could have* made a bonfire.

Inconsistency in tenses

Another common error is illogically mixing tenses within a sentence or within an entire piece of writing. Choose the tense you want to use in your sentence or in your essay and then make certain that all verbs are consistent with it, either by being in the same tense or by reflecting past and future times in relation to your main tense.

> Robertson *went* into the market, *walks* over to the produce section, and *picks* through the tomatoes. (inconsistent tenses)

In the preceding sentence there is no logical reason to move from the past tense (*went*) to the present tense (*walks, picks*). Use the past tense or the present tense—not both. Rewrite the sentence using consistent tenses.

> Robertson *went* into the market, *walked* over to the produce section, and *picked* through the tomatoes. (consistent tenses)

Look at the tenses in this group of sentences.

> Unlike Richardson's, this program *will pay* its own way. It *specified* that anyone who *wanted* to use the service *has to pay* a fee. People who *refused* to do so *won't* receive the benefits. (inconsistent tenses)

Notice that the changes in tense between sentences are not related to a clear time sequence. A rewritten version of this piece shows a more consistent, logical use of tenses.

> Unlike Richardson's, this program *will pay* its own way. It *specifies* that anyone who *wants* to use the service *has to pay* a fee. People who *refuse* to do so *won't* receive the benefits. (consistent tenses)

In this version, all verb tenses except the first (*will pay*) and last (*won't receive* = *will not receive*) are in the present tense. The future tense is appropriately used for the first and last verbs because these verbs indicate future consequences.

Irregular verbs

Even when you understand the correct uses of tenses, you can run into trouble with verbs. The major culprit is the large group of irregular verbs, which form the past tense and past participle in a variety of ways (as in Table 2-12), not by adding *-d* or *-ed* as regular verbs do.

Table 2-12

	Regular verbs	*Irregular verbs*
Present:	*talk, joke*	
Present:		*say, bite*
Past:	*talked, joked*	
Past:		*said, bit*
Past Participle:	*have talked,*	
Past Participle:		*have said, have joked*
		have bitten

Irregular verbs cause errors simply because people aren't sure about the correct past and past participle forms: Which is it? "I *drunk* the beer" or "I *drank* the beer"? Table 2-13 is a list of fifty commonly used irregular verbs with their past tenses and past participles. However, there are many others, so when you aren't sure about a verb, check the dictionary. The entry will include the verb's principal parts: present, past, and past participle.

Table 2-13   Common Irregular Verbs

Present Tense	*Past Tense*	*Past Participle*
be	was, were	(have) been
beat	beat	(have) beaten, beat
begin	began	(have)begun
blow	blew	(have) blown

(continued)

Table 2-13 *(continued)*

Present Tense	Past Tense	Past Participle
break	broke	(have) broken
bring	brought	(have) brought
catch	caught	(have) caught
choose	chose	(have) chosen
come	came	(have) come
dig	dug	(have) dug
dive	dived, dove	(have) dived
do	did	(have) done
draw	drew	(have) drawn
dream	dreamed, dreamt	(have) dreamed, dreamt
drink	drank	(have) drunk
drive	drove	(have) driven
eat	ate	(have) eaten
fly	flew	(have) flown
forget	forgot	(have) forgotten
freeze	froze	(have) frozen
get	got	(have) gotten
go	went	(have) gone
grow	grew	(have) grown
hang (an object)	hung	(have) hung
hang (a person)	hanged	(have) hanged
lay	laid	(have) laid
lead	led	(have) led
lend	lent	(have) lent
lie (recline)	lay	(have) lain
light	lighted, lit	(have) lighted, lit
ride	rode	(have) ridden
ring	rang	(have) rung
run	ran	(have) run

Present Tense	Past Tense	Past Participle
see	saw	(have) seen
set	set	(have) set
shake	shook	(have) shaken
shine (emit light)	shone	(have) shone
shine (make shiny)	shone, shined	(have) shone, shined
sing	sang	(have) sung
sink	sank, sunk	(have) sunk
slay	slew	(have) slain
speed	sped	(have) sped
spring	sprang, sprung	(have) sprung
steal	stole	(have) stolen
swear	swore	(have) sworn
swim	swam	(have) swum
take	took	(have) taken
tear	tore	(have) torn
wake	waked, woke	(have) waked, woke, woken
wear	wore	(have) worn

Chapter Checkout

Q&A

1. Identify the following verbs as active or passive voice.

    a. The song <u>was sung</u> by my favorite group.

    b. The exam <u>was</u> hard.

    c. *Beloved* <u>was written</u> by Toni Morrison.

2. Write in the principal parts of each of the following verbs.

Present	Present perfect	Past perfect	Future perfect
a. know	_____	_____	_____
b. want	_____	_____	_____
c. catch	_____	_____	_____

3. Identify the underlined verb tense.

   a. Emily <u>will have lost</u> ten pounds by spring.
   b. Susie, determined to see the world, <u>went</u> to Alaska.
   c. I <u>had gone</u> before Yassine arrived.
   d. Lillie, a master gardener, <u>will plant</u> beans next year.

4. Supply the missing verb for the following sentences. The appropriate verb is provided in parentheses.

   a. Jerome and Theresa _____ five years this November. (marry)
   b. Don _____ to New Orleans last February. (go)
   c. Mother _____ when she sees what Erik has done. (proud)
   d. We are grateful for the customers who _____us this year. (support)

5. True or False: The following underlined verbs are all action verbs.

   a. David <u>called</u> on Friday.
   b. <u>Stop</u>!
   c. Peggy <u>was</u> never late for class.

Answers: 1. a. passive b. active c. passive 2. a. have known/has known, had known, will have known b. have wanted/has wanted, had wanted, will have wanted c. have caught/has caught, had caught, will have caught 3. a. future perfect b. past c. past perfect d. future 4. a. have been married b. went c. will be proud d. have supported. 5. a. false b. true c. false.

Chapter 3
PRONOUNS

Chapter Check-In

❏ Identifying pronouns

❏ Knowing when to use subjective or objective case

❏ Making pronoun references clear

❏ Creating pronoun agreement

❏ Avoiding sexist pronouns

A pronoun is a part of speech that can be used to replace a noun. There are many different kinds of pronouns: personal, reflexive, demonstrative, relative, interrogative, and indefinite.

Case is the way pronouns are used in a sentence, and this can be subjective, objective, or possessive. Choosing between the subjective and objective case can be confusing, for example, the choice of who or whom. Pronouns always clearly refer to their antecedents, the noun they represent and they also agree with their antecedents in number and gender. If you can use pronouns with confidence, your writing will be clearer and easier to read.

The Pronoun

A **pronoun** allows flexibility in writing because it is a word that stands for a noun. Without pronouns, writing and speech would sound unnatural and boring. Compare the following two sentences.

Charlie left *Charlie's* house, taking *Charlie's* dog with *Charlie.*

Charlie left *his* house, taking *his* dog with *him.*

Obviously, the second sentence is much better. Dividing pronouns into groups based on what they do is helpful in showing how many purposes they serve.

Personal pronouns

The **personal pronouns** *(I, me, he, she, it,* etc.) stand for one or more persons or things and differ in form depending on their **case,** that is, how they are used in a phrase, clause, or sentence. For example, when acting as a subject, the first person singular pronoun is *I.* When acting as an object, *I* becomes *me.*

Reflexive (intensive) pronouns

The **reflexive,** or **intensive, pronouns** combine some of the personal pronouns with *-self* or *-selves* (*myself, himself, themselves,* etc.). Reflexive pronouns are used to reflect nouns or pronouns, as in *He hurt himself,* or to provide emphasis, as in *I myself don't believe it.* Don't use reflexive pronouns as subjects and objects, however.

> Tom and *I* don't like it.
> NOT   Tom and *myself* don't like it.

> Bob doesn't like Harold or *me.*
> NOT   Bob doesn't like Harold or *myself.*

Demonstrative pronouns

The **demonstrative pronouns** *(this, that, these, those)* single out what you are talking about.

> *These* are the ones we want, but *this* is the most economical choice.

When they stand alone in place of nouns, these words are pronouns. But when they precede nouns, they are adjectives: *this wagon, that dog, these words.*

Relative pronouns

The **relative pronouns** *(who, whom, which, that)* introduce clauses that describe nouns or pronouns.

> The professor *who wrote the textbook* is teaching the class.
> The storm *that caused the blackout* has moved east.

Relative clauses are discussed in detail in Chapter 6.

The current trend is toward using the relative pronouns *that* and *which* interchangeably, although many teachers and editors prefer that a distinction be made. Use *that* when the clause that follows it is *restrictive,* that is, when it is necessary to define your subject. Use *which* when the clause that follows it is *nonrestrictive,* that is, when it adds information that isn't necessary to define your subject. For a complete explanation of restrictive and non-restrictive clauses, see Chapter 9.

> The car *that hit her* was green.
> NOT The car *which hit her* was green.

The relative clause *that hit her* restricts or limits the subject car. The information in the clause is necessary to the main statement.

> The car, *which I bought a week ago,* gets good mileage.
> NOT The car, *that I bought a week ago,* gets good mileage.

The clause *which I bought a week ago* adds information about the subject that isn't necessary to our understanding of the main statement that the car gets good mileage.

Use commas with a *which* clause but not with a *that* clause. (See Chapter 9 for commas with restrictive and nonrestrictive clauses.)

Interrogative pronouns

The **interrogative pronouns** *(who whom, whose, which, what)* introduce questions.

> *Which* is the best one to choose?
> *Who* asked the question, "To *whom* does this belong?"

Indefinite pronouns

Indefinite pronouns don't specify the persons or things they refer to. The most frequently used indefinite pronouns are all, any, anybody, anyone, both, each, either, everybody, everyone, few, many, neither, nobody, none, no one, one, several, some, somebody, someone. There are many others (for example, others here is an indefinite pronoun). Like other pronouns (here, other is an adjective), indefinite pronouns stand in for nouns, even if those nouns aren't specified.

> *Many* are called but *few* are chosen.
> *Nobody* likes a tattletale.

Pronoun Case

Case refers to the way a noun or pronoun is used in a sentence. When it is the subject of a verb, it is in the **subjective case** (the term nominative can also be used for subjective case though we will use subjective case only). When it is the object of a verb or a preposition, it is in the **objective case.**

When it possesses something, it is in the **possessive case.**

With nouns, the subjective and objective cases aren't a problem because nouns have the same form whether they are subjects or objects.

The *frog* ate the *bee.* The *bee* stung the *frog.*

Regardless of what's happening to the frog or the bee, the nouns *frog* and *bee* don't change form.

Some pronouns, however, take different forms depending on whether they are subjects or objects. These pronouns are listed in Table 3-1.

Table 3-1: Subjective and objective pronouns

Subjective case	Objective case
I	me
he	him
she	her
we	us
they	them
who, whoever	whom, whomever

In the sentence *Tension existed between Franklin and Winston,* there is no confusion about what case to use for *Franklin* or *Winston.* But what about in this sentence?

Tension existed between Franklin and *him.*

Is *him* right? Or should it be *he?* (The pronoun is the object of the preposition *between,* so *him* is correct.).

Subjective case of pronouns

Pronouns are used as subjects of verbs. Use the subjective case of pronouns when the pronoun is the subject of a verb.

I drive to work.

He enjoys dancing.

We bought the lodge.

They are fighting over the property line.

The man *who won* the game was the guest of honor.

Compound subjects

When there are **compound subjects,** that is, more than one actor, don't be confused. Pronouns should still be in the subjective case.

> *Eileen and he* (NOT *Eileen and him*) enjoy dancing.
>
> *The Harrisons and they* (NOT *The Harrisons and them*) are fighting over the property line.

To keep from making pronoun case errors in sentences with compound subjects, drop the subject that is a noun and read the sentence with the pronoun alone. You would never say *Him enjoy dancing* or *Them are fighting over the property line.* You'll see immediately that the subjective forms *he* and *they* are correct.

Pronouns following "to be"

You should also use the subjective case of pronouns after forms of the verb *to be.*

> It *is I* who chose the location.
>
> The man who called the police *was he.*
>
> The real criminals *are we* ourselves.
>
> The winners *were they* and the Rudermans.
>
> The man who phoned *was who?*

The word after a form of *to be* is called a **complement.** (It is also sometimes called a *predicate nominative* or *predicate adjective).*

Unlike words following action verbs, a complement of a linking verb is not an object, a receiver of action. Instead, the complement identifies or refers to the subject. Compare the following two sentences.

> The president *saw Mr. Komine.*
>
> The president *was Mr. Komine.*

In the first sentence, *Mr. Komine* is an object that receives the president's action of seeing. If a pronoun were to be substituted for *Mr. Komine,* the pronoun would be in the objective case: *him.* But in the second sentence, *Mr. Komine* isn't receiving any action; *Mr. Komine* identities the subject, that is, the president. The correct pronoun to substitute for *Mr. Komine* in this sentence would be *he.*

Pronoun complements can cause case problems. As the rule says, the subjective form of a pronoun is correct after *to be,* but sometimes it may sound unnatural or awkwardly formal.

It is *I.*

I am *she.*

The person I chose was *he.*

The winners were *they.*

The best way to handle awkward-sounding constructions is to look for a better way to say the same thing. For example,

> They were the winners.

OR They won. (better)

> He was the person I chose.

OR I chose him. (better)

In informal speech and writing, modern usage allows *It is me* or *It's me.* Objective pronouns after *to be* are also gaining some acceptance in other constructions. When you are writing formally, either stay with the established rule or rewrite the sentence to avoid an awkward correctness.

Objective Case of Pronouns

When a pronoun is the object of the verb or preposition it is in the objective case. (See Chapter 2 for direct and indirect objects.)

Pronouns as objects of verbs

Use the objective case of pronouns when the pronoun is a direct or indirect object of a verb.

> Gilbertson *nominated me* for secretary. (direct object of *nominated)*

> The news *hit them* hard. (direct object of *hit)*

> Jennifer *gave him* the house and car. (indirect object of *gave)*

> Robert Chang *told us* and *them* the same incredible story. (indirect objects of *told)*

Pronouns as objects of prepositions

You should also use the objective case of pronouns when the pronoun is an object of a preposition. (Prepositions are discussed in detail in Chapter 5.)

> The man pulled a blanket *over* the children and *us.* (object of the preposition *over)*

> The man *for whom* they waited never arrived. (They waited *for whom:* object of the preposition *for)*

Pronoun over-refinement

Choosing *between you and me* vs. *between you and I* should be easy. Some people incorrectly believe that the subjective forms are more correct—that *I* is actually superior to *me*. Where this idea comes from is a mystery—perhaps from having *It's me* corrected to *It is I* or from recognizing obvious bad grammar, as in *Me and him really like you*. But don't be influenced by a misguided idea of refinement. The objective case has a clear purpose as the rules show, and not to use it when you should reveals your lack of knowledge. The phrase for *You and I* and *between you and I* are common mistakes that are probably due to over-refinement. The pronouns in these phrases are objects of prepositions, and therefore for *you and me* and *between you and me* are correct.

Compound objects

Watch out for pronoun case when you have a compound object. Remember that when an object is more than one person, it is still an object. Pronouns should be in the objective case.

> The ceremony will be given for *Tucker, Martinez, and me*. (NOT *for Tucker, Martinez, and I*)
>
> *Without Kate and me* (NOT *Without Kate and I*), the book wouldn't have been published.
>
> The dean *nominated Nelson and me* (NOT *Nelson and I*) to serve on the committee.

You can check for pronoun cases in such situations by reading the sentences with the pronoun object alone: *The ceremony will be given for I; Without I, the book wouldn't have been published; The dean nominated I to serve on the committee.* The mistakes show up quickly. *Me* is obviously the right form of the pronoun in these three sentences.

Pronouns as subjects of infinitives

When a pronoun is the subject of an infinitive (the basic verb with *to: to swim, to drive,* etc.), use the objective case for the pronoun. This rule shouldn't cause you any problems. Your ear will tell you the objective case is correct.

> He wanted *her to drive* the car.
>
> Bradford liked *them to leave* early.

Choosing Between the Subjective and Objective Case

Choosing between the subjective and objective case is sometimes complicated by appositives, and the *as* or *than* construction. The confusion over the choice of *who* or *whom* is a good example of this problem.

Pronoun case with appositives

An **appositive** is a word or group of words that restates or identifies the noun or pronoun it is next to: My sister *Hephzibah;* John, *the gardener,* our friend *Carlos;* We, *the people.* The presence of an appositive doesn't change the rule for pronoun case; that is, use the subjective case for subjects and the objective case for objects.

> The decision to close the pool was a setback for *us swimmers.* (NOT *we swimmers*)

The best way to make sure you have chosen the correct pronoun case is to read the sentence without the appositive: *The decision to close the pool was a setback for we.* Once again, you can see immediately that *us* is the right pronoun to use.

Pronoun case after *as, than.* Choosing the right pronoun case after *as* or *than* can be difficult.

Look at the following two sentences.

> You respect Professor Morrow more *than I.*
> You respect Professor Morrow more *than me.*

Depending on the meaning, either choice could be correct. If the writer means *You respect Professor Morrow more than I (respect Professor Morrow),* then the first sentence is correct. If the writer means *You respect Professor Morrow more than (you respect) me,* then the second sentence is correct.

The key to choosing the right pronoun case is to supply mentally the missing part of the clause.

> Did you work as hard *as they?* (*worked*)
> I like Ed better *than he.* (*likes* Ed)
> I like Ed better *than him.* (*than I like him*)
> They are smarter *than we.* (*are*)

If a sentence sounds awkward to you—for example, *They are smarter than we*—you can avoid the problem by actually supplying the missing word: *They are smarter than we are.*

Who, whom, whoever, whomever

These pronouns cause so much anxiety that they are being treated separately, even though the rules about case are the same as those for *I, he, she, we,* and *they.*

As a subject, choose *who* or *whoever.*

> He was the man *who won* the game. (subject of *won*)
>
> *Whoever wants* the paper can have it. (subject of *wants*)

As an object, choose *whom* or *whomever.*

> He was a person *around whom* controversy swirled. (object of the preposition *around*)
>
> *Whomever will* you *invite?* (You *will invite whomever:* direct object)

In informal speech and writing *whom is* used infrequently. At the beginning of questions, for example, *who* is substituted for *whom,* even when *whom* would be grammatically correct.

> *Who* will you marry? (You will marry *whom.*)
>
> *Who* did he ask? (He did ask *whom.*)

Even some standardized tests have given up *who/whom questions.* Who knows? Maybe *whom will* disappear from the language someday. Does this mean you should feel free to ignore it? Probably not yet, at least in formal writing. It is still safer to maintain the distinction between *who* and *whom*—and maintain it correctly.

Possessive Case of Pronouns

The possessive case of nouns is formed with an apostrophe: *Keesha's* costume, *the wolf's fangs* (See Chapter 1). But personal pronouns and the relative pronoun *who* change form to indicate possession.

> *My house* is bigger than *your house.*
>
> *His anger* evaporated in the face of *her explanation.*
>
> The bulldog bared *its teeth* at us.
>
> *Our decision* affected *their* plans.
>
> The economist, *whose book* had received good reviews, agreed to speak.
>
> No mother tried harder to help than *hers.*
>
> *Your plans* are more definite than *ours.*

Remember that possessive-case nouns and pronouns are different; possessive pronouns do not have apostrophes. You have to distinguish between *its, it's,* and *whose, who's.* The possessive of *it* is *its,* NOT *it's;* the possessive of *who* is *whose,* NOT *who's. It's* and *who's* are contractions *(it's = it is; who's = who is).*

> The cat lost *its whiskers.* (NOT *it's whiskers*)
>
> *It's (It is)* Friday!
>
> The boy *whose mother* (NOT *who's mother*) called left the meeting.
>
> *Who's (Who is)* the author of the book?

Possessive Pronouns with Gerunds

Use a possessive pronoun with a gerund, the verb form that functions as a noun (See Chapter 1). This rule is broken frequently, with many writers using the objective rather than the possessive case.

> I didn't like *his going* (NOT *him going*) to New York without me.
>
> *Their smiling* (NOT *Them smiling*) irritated her.
>
> Please forgive *our intruding.* (NOT *us intruding*)

Pronoun Reference

Pronouns always refer to the noun they represent, their antecedent. If you understand how pronouns relate to nouns, you can avoid confusion in your writing.

Finding the antecedent

Remember that pronouns stand in for nouns. An **antecedent** is the noun—or group of words acting as a noun—that a pronoun refers to. Notice the antecedents in the following example.

> Kelly lifted *Mickey* into the air and then set *him* down.
>
> The *debt* plagued *John and Sandy. It* ruined any chance *they* had for a peaceful relationship.

Neither of these examples would make a reader wonder who or what is being talked about. *Him* in the first example is *Mickey, It* and *they* in the second example are *debt* and *John and Sandy.*

Unclear antecedents

In the following sentences, locate the antecedents of the pronouns.

> The counselor was speaking to Dave, and *he* looked unhappy.

Who looked unhappy in this sentence—the counselor or Dave? In the following sentence, did the maids clean the girls or the rooms?

> After the girls left the hotel rooms, the maids cleaned *them*.

In the second example, your good sense tells you the maids cleaned the rooms and didn't clean the girls. But although sometimes you can count on context or good sense to help you figure out which pronoun goes with which antecedent, you shouldn't have to. And what about in the first sentence? No clue exists as to whether the counselor or Dave looked unhappy. These are examples of ambiguous pronoun references, and you should avoid them in your writing.

You can solve the problem in various ways, including changing the sentence structure or eliminating the pronoun, as in the following sentences.

> The counselor was speaking to Dave, who looked unhappy.
> After the girls left, the maids cleaned the hotel rooms.

Be sure to read your sentences carefully to make sure that you have avoided unclear pronoun references.

Indefinite antecedents

More subtle errors occur when you use a pronoun reference that is too general or indefinite or one that exists only in your mind.

> I told Uncle Richard, Aunt Gretchen, and then Father, *which* infuriated Gary.

Did telling all three people infuriate Gary, or was it only telling Father? Rewrite the sentence to make your meaning clear.

> First I told Uncle Richard and Aunt Gretchen. Then I told Father, which infuriated Gary.
>
> OR My telling Uncle Richard, Aunt Gretchen, and then Father infuriated Gary.

In the following sentence, no antecedent exists for *them*. The writer is thinking "bagels" but not specifying them. *Bagel shop* is not a correct antecedent for *them*. To solve the problem, substitute *bagels* for *them*.

> Although Mark likes working at the bagel shop, he never eats *them* himself.

In the next sentence, the antecedent for *It* is vague. Was it just the sky that filled the observer with hope and joy? A hint in rewriting: Substitute *The scene* for *It*.

The hills were lush green, the trees in full bloom, the sky a brilliant blue. *It* filled me with hope and joy.

What is the exact antecedent for *This* in the following sentence?

The paper was too long, too general, and too filled with pretentious language. *This* meant Joe had to rewrite it.

A possible rewrite might be as follows.

The paper was too long, too general, and too filled with pretentious language. *These problems* meant that Joe had to rewrite it.

Don't try to remedy a vague pronoun reference by changing the pronoun, as in the following example.

The paper was too long, too general, and too filled with pretentious language, *which* meant Joe had to rewrite it.

The reference for *which* is as indefinite as was the reference for *this,* and so the problem has not been solved.

The vague *this* and the indefinite *it* are so common in writing that they often go unnoticed. *It* can be used as an indefinite indicator occasionally: *It's true, It is raining, It is a ten minute drive to the school.* But don't overdo this construction. For vivid writing, nail down your pronouns with good, clear antecedents.

Pronoun Agreement

A pronoun must agree with its antecedent in number (singular or plural) and gender (masculine or feminine).

In this sentence, *Harold* is the antecedent of *his, he'd,* and *his.*

Harold, after saying goodbye to *his* family, discovered *he'd* lost his wallet.

In the following sentence, *Garcias* is the antecedent of *they,* even though it follows the pronoun.

Until *they* buy the house, the *Garcias* are staying in a hotel.

Look at the next example. Here, *Peterson and Mancini* is a compound antecedent, which requires the plural pronoun *their.*

Peterson and Mancini took *their* cue from the senator.

Agreement problems with indefinite pronouns

Indefinite pronouns cause many agreement problems. Some pronouns (*several, few, both,* and *many*) are clearly plural and take both plural verbs and plural pronouns.

> *Several are* expected to give up *their* rooms.
>
> *Both tell their* parents the truth.

Some pronouns may *"feel"* plural, but are singular and take singular verbs and pronouns. In this group are *each, either, neither, everyone, everybody, no one, nobody, anyone, anybody, someone,* and *somebody.*

> *Each is* responsible for *his or her* (NOT *their*) own ticket.
>
> *Everyone wants* to get *his or her* (NOT *their*) name in the paper.

When the use of a singular form would lead to a statement that doesn't make sense, you should use a plural form. For example, in the sentence *Everyone left the lecture because he thought it was boring, they* would be a better choice than *he* for the pronoun. However, the general rule is to use singular forms of verbs and pronouns with these indefinite pronouns.

Some indefinite pronouns (*none, any, some, all, most*) fall into an "either/or" category; and they may take singular or plural verbs and pronouns, depending on meaning. Sometimes the distinction is subtle.

> *None* of the men *was* hurt. (*not one* = singular)
>
> *None* of the men *were* hurt. (*no men* = plural)
>
> *Some is* better than none. (*some* = a quantity = singular)
>
> *Some are* delicious. (*some* = a number of things = plural)
>
> *All is* well. (*all* = the sum of all things singular)
>
> *All are* well. (*all* = a number of people plural)

If a plural meaning is not clear from the context, use singular verbs and pronouns.

Pronouns with collective nouns

Collective nouns can also require either singular or plural verbs and singular or plural pronouns, depending on meaning.

> The *team* plays according to its schedule. (emphasize unit = singular)
>
> The *team* couldn't agree on *their* goals. (emphasize individuals = plural)

However, if you are uncertain, choose a singular verb and a singular pronoun, or rewrite the sentence to make it clearly plural.

The team *members* couldn't agree on *their* goals.

Sexism in Pronouns: *He or She?*

When the gender of a pronoun antecedent is unknown, or when the antecedent represents both sexes, which third person singular pronoun should you *use—he* or *she?* Traditionally, *he* has been the automatic choice.

The diplomatic *person* keeps *his* opinion to *himself.*

The *reader himself* will decide whether *he* wants to accept Smith's premise.

For the past several years, however, some people have objected to this one-sided view of things. But remedying it hasn't been easy, and usage experts don't agree on one solution. Here are some ways of handling the problem.

■ When possible, rewrite sentences using third person plural forms.

Diplomatic *people* keep *their* opinions to *themselves.*

■ Use *he or she.*

The *reader* will decide whether *he or she* wishes to accept Smith's premise.

■ Use *he/she* or *s/he.*

The *reader* will decide whether *he/she* (or *s/he*) wishes to accept Smith's premise.

■ Continue to use *he* throughout a piece of writing.

■ Use *she* instead of *he* throughout a piece of writing.

■ Alternate between *he* and *she* within a piece of writing.

■ Use *their* even when the antecedent is singular.

A *ticket holder* must check *their* number.

This book recommends using third person plural whenever that solution is possible and *he or she* when the plural form is awkward or inappropriate. However, constant repetition of *he or she* slows the flow of a sentence, and you risk annoying your reader if you use the phrase too often.

The solutions aren't ideal, but they seem less likely to offend than choosing either *he* or *she* exclusively and less confusing than alternating between them. The recommended solutions also prevent your being accused of making a grammatical blunder by using a plural pronoun with a singular antecedent (choice 7). Finally, *he or she* is preferable to the bureaucratic-sounding *he/she* or the unpronounceable *s/he*.

Chapter Checkout

Q&A

1. Choose the correct pronoun to complete the sentences.

   a. Nicole and <u>she/her</u> bought a new car.
   b. The teacher who fell was <u>who/whom</u>?
   c. He never knew that it was <u>I/me</u> who loved him.
   d. The dolphin swam under the trainer and <u>I/me</u>.
   e. My aunt knitted a sweater for Joan and <u>she/her</u>.
   f. The president for <u>who/whom</u> we voted won.

2. In the following sentences identify the pronoun and state whether it is demonstrative, interrogative, relative, or reflexive.

   a. Which is the better bargain?
   b. Celia braced herself for the winter blast.
   c. That was James's greatest achievement.
   d. The author who lived in Memphis has died.

3. Underline the pronouns in the following sentences and label them subjective, possessive, or objective.

   a. Melinda had read the book, and she anticipated the movie.
   b. With the exception of the conductor, no one saw them arrive.
   c. When the rose bloomed in November, it was lovely.
   d. That mug is mine.

Answers: 1. a. she b. who c. I d. me e. her f. whom 2. a. which, interrogative b. herself, reflexive c. That, demonstrative d. who, relative. 3. a. she, subjective b. them, objective c. it, subjective d. mine, possessive.

Chapter 4

MODIFIERS: ADJECTIVES AND ADVERBS

Chapter Check-In

❑ Using adjectives and adverbs

❑ Distinguishing between adjectives and adverbs

❑ Avoiding problems with adjectives and adverbs

❑ Showing degree with comparatives and superlatives

Adjectives and adverbs are parts of speech commonly called modifiers. An adjective modifies a noun or pronoun and an adverb modifies a verb, adjective, or another adverb.

Some adjectives and adverbs require memorizing a few rules. For example, *bad* is always used as an adjective, while *badly* is an adverb. Adjectives and adverbs can also be used to show comparative or superlative degree. By adding *-er* you can compare two people, things, or an action, or by adding *-est* you can compare more than two things. You can make your sentences more precise and interesting by using appropriate adjectives and adverbs.

The Modifier

A **modifier** describes or limits another word or group of words. To correctly identify the modifier as an adjective or adverb, it is important to identify the word the adjective or adverb is modifying.

An **adjective** modifies a noun or pronoun. In the following sentence, *orange* is an adjective modifying the noun *curtains,* and *cool* is an adjective modifying the noun *breeze.*

The *orange* curtains billowed in the *cool* breeze.

In the next example, *happy* is an adjective modifying the pronoun *I;* this kind of adjective, one following a linking verb, is called a predicate adjective. *Thoughtful* is an adjective modifying the noun *gesture.*

I am *happy* because of his *thoughtful* gesture.

An **adverb** modifies a verb, an adjective, or another adverb. Adverbs answer questions such as *how, how much, when, where,* and *why.* In the following sentence, *sadly* modifies the verb *smiled* and answers the question "How did he smile?"

He smiled *sadly.*

In the next example, *immediately* answers the question "When did they come?"

They came *immediately.*

Here answers the question "Where did she walk?"

She walked *here.*

Very modifies the adjective *bright:* "How bright were the curtains?"

The orange curtains were *very* bright.

Remarkably modifies the adverb *quickly:* "How quickly did he crawl?"

He crawled *remarkably* quickly.

When to Use Modifiers

Adjectives and adverbs don't form the core of sentences as nouns and verbs do, but they give sentences texture and precision. Without adjectives and adverbs, you wouldn't know what color the curtains were, how the man crawled, when they came, etc. Use adjectives and adverbs when they make a contribution to what you are saying. For example, in "He smiled *sadly,*" you know his smile is not like the usual happy smile. *Sadly* performs a function. On the other hand, in "He screamed *loudly,*" does the adverb add anything to the verb? Is there such a thing as a soft or quiet scream? Here, loudly is unnecessary. Avoid using adjectives and adverbs that don't tell us anything or that state the obvious.

Recognizing adjectives and adverbs

Adverbs often end in *-ly* (*remarkably, quickly, happily, slowly*), but not always (*here, there, fast, late, hard*). And some adjectives end in *-ly* (a *lively* child, *friendly* dog, *hilly* area). The lesson to be learned from these examples is that to decide whether a word is an adjective or an adverb, look not at the word itself but at what the word modifies: Adjectives will always modify nouns and pronouns, while adverbs modify verbs, adjectives, and other adverbs. Review these examples.

In the following example, *old* and *red* are adjectives modifying the noun *barn.*

> The *old red* barn needs repairs.

In the next sentence, *very* is an adverb modifying the adjective old, not the noun *barn.*

> The *very* old red barn needs repairs.

Hard is an adverb modifying the verb *worked.*

> He worked *hard* all afternoon.

Here, *hard* is an adjective modifying the noun *work.*

> The *hard* work took all afternoon.

Using adjectives after linking verbs

It's natural to associate adverbs rather than adjectives with verbs; adverbs modify verbs. But with linking verbs such as *be, become, smell, taste, seem,* and *look* (see "Linking Verbs," Chapter 2), use adjectives (called predicate adjectives).

> The substance tastes *sweet.* (NOT *sweetly*)
> They were *joyful.* (NOT *joyfully*)

Notice the use of adjectives or adverbs in the following sentences, depending on whether a verb is functioning as a linking verb or an action verb.

In the following example, *grow* is an action verb meaning *to develop, increase in size,* and its modifier should be an adverb *(beautifully).*

> Flowers *grow beautifully* in that climate.

Here, *grow* is a linking verb meaning *to become,* so the complement should be an adjective *(beautiful).*

> Bronze *grows beautiful* as it ages.

In the next example, *smells* is a linking verb and takes an adjective; that is, the dog's odor is unpleasant.

> The dog *smells bad.*

Here, *smells* is an action verb and takes an adverb; that is, something is wrong with the dog's sense of smell.

> The dog smells *badly*.

Problem adjectives and adverbs

Some adjectives and adverbs seem interchangeable but are not. You will need to remember a few rules to distinguish how they are used.

Good, well. *Good* is always an adjective: *good* bread; *good* vibrations; dinner was *good*. Don't use *good* as an adverb. Use *well,* an adverb meaning to perform capably.

> She sings *well*.
> NOT She sings *good*.

> He listens *well*.
> NOT He listens *good*.

Some confusion arises between *good* and *well* because *well* can also be used as an adjective meaning *in good health*.

> Mother was *well* in time for the play.
> NOT Mother was *good* in time for the play.

To see the distinction between *well* used as an adjective and *good* used as an adjective, look at the following sentences, both with the linking verb *looked*.

> Jerome looked *good* at the party tonight. (Jerome looked attractive.)
> Jerome looked *well* at the party tonight. (Jerome looked to be in good health.)

Bad, badly. *Bad is* an adjective and *badly* is an adverb. They are often used incorrectly for each other.

> I feel *bad* about his losing the election.
> NOT I feel *badly* about his losing the election.

Here, *feel* is a linking verb and should be followed by an adjective, not an adverb. In the next examples, *badly* is an adverb describing how the team played.

> The soccer team played *badly* in the last game.
> NOT The soccer team played *bad* in the last game.

In the following sentence, the adjective *bad* follows a linking verb, so the appearance of the faucet is being discussed.

The faucet looked *bad.*

When the adverb *badly* follows the action verb, it explains how seriously the faucet leaked.

The faucet leaked *badly.*

Most, almost. *Most* is an adjective meaning *the greatest in number, amount.*

Most people agree that exercise is good for you.

Most crimes go unpunished.

But *most* is an adverb when it is used to form the superlative of an adjective:

She is the *most* intelligent woman in the group.

He is the *most* appealing when he first wakes up.

Almost is always an adverb. It means *nearly. Almost* modifies the adjectives *every* and *all. Most* cannot be used to modify *every* and *all.*

Almost every person agreed.

NOT *Most* every person agreed.

Almost all the people came.

NOT *Most* all the people came.

Forming the Comparative and Superlative Degrees

As shown in Table 4-1, adjectives and adverbs change to show the **comparative degree** and **superlative degree.**

Table 4-1

Positive degree	Comparative degree	Superlative degree
sweet (adjective)	sweeter	sweetest
sweetly (adverb)	more sweetly	most sweetly

Follow these simple rules in forming comparative and superlative with adverbs and adjectives.

Use the comparative degree when you are comparing two people, things, or actions.

> Oranges are *sweeter* than apples.
> Naomi sings *more sweetly* than Kate.

Use the superlative degree when you are comparing more than two. The superlative degree puts the modified word over all the others in its group.

> The strawberries are *sweeter* than the apples, but the oranges are *sweetest of* all.
> Of all the members of the choir, Naomi sings *most sweetly.*

Most one-syllable and some two-syllable adjectives form the comparative and superlative degrees by adding *-er* or *-est.* Notice that the adjective's final consonant is sometimes doubled and that a *-y* is changed to *-i: tall, taller, tallest; smart, smarter, smartest; big, bigger, biggest; dry, drier, driest; happy, happier, happiest.* There are a few exceptions to the rule: *good, better, best; bad, worse, worst.* If an adjective has two or more syllables, it usually forms the comparative and superlative degrees with *more* and *most: more intelligent, most intelligent; more difficult, most difficult.*

Most adverbs form the comparative and superlative forms with more and most: more slowly, most slowly, more gracefully, most gracefully; more quickly, most quickly. A few are exceptions: hard, harder, hardest; fast, faster, fastest; soon, sooner, soonest.

Be careful not to double your comparisons when you form degrees of adjectives: *funny, funnier* (NOT *more funnier), funniest* (NOT *most funniest).* To use the *-er, -est* forms with *more, most* is redundant and incorrect.

Whenever you aren't sure about how to form the comparative and superlative of a particular adjective or adverb, check your dictionary.

Adjectives and Adverbs that Should Not be Compared

Be aware that there are some adjectives and adverbs that should not be compared because of their meanings. One of the most frequently mis-compared adjectives is *unique,* meaning *one of a kind.* Something cannot be *more unique* or *most unique.* Something is either *one of a kind* or it isn't. Adjectives like this (and their adverbial forms) are absolute; *absolute* itself is an absolute adjective. Among others to watch out for are *essential,* meaning *absolutely necessary; universal,* meaning *present everywhere;* and *immortal,* meaning *living forever.* With these adjectives and adverbs, something either is or it isn't, and therefore comparative degrees are meaningless.

Chapter Checkout

Q&A

1. Identify the following underlined words as either adjectives or adverbs.

   a. The sunset faded <u>slowly</u> over the horizon.
   b. The <u>oily</u> driveway was dangerous.
   c. Myrta's <u>golden</u> hair is lovely.
   d. The driveway was a <u>little</u> rocky.
   e. Audelle took a <u>little</u> walk.

2. Choose the correct adjective or adverb to complete the sentences.

   a. My grandmother Dorothy's pie tastes <u>good/well</u>.
   b. Ahmed plays the cello <u>well/good</u>.
   c. Although he said he was feeling better, Tony did not look <u>good/well</u>.
   d. Because she missed his birthday, Judy felt <u>bad/badly</u>.
   e. <u>Most/Almost</u> all the tourists attended the musical.
   f. <u>Most/Almost</u> statistics prove otherwise.
   g. He was the <u>good/better/best</u> of the two players.
   h. He is the <u>smart/smarter/smartest</u> student in the class.
   i. That was a <u>perfect/more perfect/most perfect</u> day.

3. Provide the comparative and superlative degree for the following adjectives and adverbs.

   a. late
   b. easily
   c. happy
   d. far
   e. sorrowfully

Answers: 1. a. adverb b. adjective c. adjective d. adverb e. adjective
2. a. good b. well c. well d. bad e. Almost f. Most g. better h. smartest
i. perfect 3. a. later, latest b. easier, easiest c. happier, happiest d. farther,
farthest e. more sorrowfully, most sorrowfully.

Chapter 5

PREPOSITIONS, CONJUNCTIONS, AND INTERJECTIONS

Prepositions, conjunctions and interjections are the connecting elements in sentences. Finding the link between words is the secret to identifying prepositions. The two most important rules about using prepositions are avoid using excess prepositions and avoid ending sentences with prepositions.

Conjunctions are parts of speech that connect words, phrases, or clauses. There are three types of conjunctions: coordinating, correlative, and subordinating. They are the key to logically constructed sentences.

Interjections are used to express powerful or sudden emotion and are usually not grammatically connected to any other sentence. While there are no formal rules for interjections, they are most effective if used sparingly.

The Preposition

A **preposition** shows the relationship between a noun or pronoun and another noun or pronoun.

> The cat *under* the <u>fence</u>.
> The cat *between* the <u>fence</u> and the <u>house</u>.
> Everyone *except* the <u>girl</u> *in* the blue dress.
> A letter *about* <u>us</u>.

The italicized words in the preceding phrases are prepositions; the underlined words are **objects of the prepositions.** When the object is a pronoun, remember that the pronoun should be in the objective case (see Chapter 3).

Recognizing prepositions

How do you recognize a preposition? It's sometimes not easy. Prepositions aren't as obvious as nouns and verbs. Look for a word that establishes a certain kind of relationship with another word. For example, in the previous phrases, how is *cat* related to *fence?* The cat is *under* the fence. How is *Everyone* related to the *girl?* The *girl* is left out of the group *Everyone.* How is *girl* related to *dress?* She is *in* it. Table 5-1 shows several words commonly used as prepositions.

Table 5-1   Words Commonly Used as Prepositions

about	before	down	off	under
above	behind	during	on	underneath
across	below	except	out	until
after	beneath	for	over	unto
against	beside	from	past	up
along	between	in	since	upon
among	beyond	into	through	with
around	by	like	to	within
at	concerning	of	toward	without

Some prepositions, called **compound prepositions,** are made up of more than one word, such as *according to, because of, in front of, instead of, in spite of,* and *next to.*

Confusing use of prepositions

The unnecessary use of prepositions is a common error. Be careful not to use a preposition where it isn't needed.

> Where have you been?
>
> NOT Where have you been *at?*

> Where is Robert going?
>
> NOT Where is Robert going *to?*

Also, don't use two prepositions when you need only one.

> Don't go *near* the water
>
> NOT Don't go *near to* the water.
>
> The book fell *off* the table.
>
> NOT The book fell *off of* the table.

Ending a sentence with a preposition can cause problems. The rule that a sentence should never end with a preposition is no longer strictly enforced. Still, many writers avoid ending sentences with prepositions, which is generally a good idea. But use your own judgment. If you feel ending with a preposition makes a particular sentence more natural, do so and don't worry about it.

> It is a comment *to which* I will not respond.
>
> COMPARED TO It is a comment I will not respond *to*.
>
> I bought a pen *with which* to write.
>
> COMPARED TO I bought a pen to write *with*.

Defining Conjunctions

Conjunctions are words that join or link elements. Like prepositions, they get a job done rather than add excitement to your writing. But choosing the right conjunction makes the logic of your thought clear. For example, which of the following two sentences creates the more logical connection?

> I've always disliked history, *and* I have never failed a test.
>
> I've always disliked history, *but* I have never failed a test.

Because the two clauses suggest contradictory ideas, *but* provides a more logical connection than *and*.

Coordinating conjunctions

The **coordinating conjunctions** are *and, but, for, nor, or, so,* and *yet.* These conjunctions join words, phrases, or clauses that are grammatically equal in rank.

> Words: *Mother and daughter, tea and toast*
>
> Phrases: We found the Easter eggs *under the couch and in the closet.*
>
> Clauses: *He likes me, but I don't care.*

Each clause *(He likes me* and *I don't care)* can stand alone. The two clauses are grammatically equal.

Correlative conjunctions

Correlative conjunctions are like coordinating conjunctions except that they come in matched pairs: *either/or, neither/nor, both/and, not only/ but also,* and *whether/or.*

> Words: *Neither mother nor daughter*
>
> Phrases: We found the Easter eggs *not only under the couch but also in the closet.*
>
> Clauses: *Either you surrender or I shoot.*

For maintaining parallel construction when using correlative conjunctions, see Chapter 7.

Subordinating conjunctions

Subordinating conjunctions join unequal elements. A subordinating conjunction joins a clause that can't stand alone (called a **subordinate** or **dependent clause**) to a clause that can (called an **independent clause**). Clauses are discussed in more detail in Chapter 6.

> We will discontinue research in this area *unless* the results of the experiment are promising.

The clause beginning with *unless* cannot stand alone; it is subordinate to, or dependent on, the independent clause *We will discontinue research in this area. Unless* is the subordinating conjunction that links the two clauses.

> The train arrived *before* we did.

Before we did is a dependent clause; it cannot stand alone. It depends on the independent clause *The train arrived. Before* is the subordinating conjunction that links the clauses.

Table 5-2 includes some words that can act as subordinating conjunctions.

Table 5-2   Words That Can Act as Subordinating Conjunctions

after	before	than	whenever
although	even if	that	where
as	if	though	wherever
as if	in order that	till	while
as long as	provided (that)	unless	
as though	since	until	
because	so (that)	when	

You may notice that some of these words were also on the list of prepositions. Once again, remember that a word's part of speech depends on its function, not on the word itself. A preposition shows a relationship between words and has an object, whereas a subordinating conjunction joins a dependent clause to an independent one.

The man stood hesitantly *before* the door.

In the preceding sentence, *before* is a preposition; its object is *door.* The preposition shows the relationship between the man and the door.

Before the expedition can begin, the details must be addressed.

Here, *before* is a subordinating conjunction, linking the dependent clause *Before the expedition can begin* to the independent clause *the details must be addressed.*

Using Interjections

Oh! The joy of **interjections!** Interjections, words that express a burst of emotion, are not grammatically related to other elements in a sentence.

Hey! Gadzooks! Oh, no! Bravo! Whoopee!

Curses are also interjections: *Damn!*

Interjections can add a sudden and emotional tone to your writing if they are used judiciously. The good news is that no rules apply to interjections. The bad news is that you should limit your use of them, particularly in formal writing. Even in informal writing the power of interjections will be diluted if they are used too often. Generally, although not always, exclamation points immediately follow interjections.

Ouch! Hurrah! Mercy!
Ah, to be in Paris in the spring!

Chapter Checkout

Q&A

1. Identify the preposition and the object of the preposition in the following sentences.
   a. Ivy grew between the bricks.
   b. Within a year, Tom will be an architect.
   c. The squirrels played beneath my window.

2. True or False: All of the following sentences are grammatically correct uses of prepositions.

   a. Would you like to come with me?
   b. Where did you graduate from?
   c. He lives near by the stream.
   d. I cannot decide between Libertarians and Democrats.
   e. I left my glasses beside of my book.
   f. He is involved by his music.
   g. Be quiet and listen at the instructions.
   h. We split the reward among three children.

3. Match the underlined word with the correct conjunction.

   a. We were surprised, <u>yet</u> we laughed.   Coordinating
   b. <u>Whenever</u> she reads, Moesha takes notes.   Correlative
   c. Not only was he cold, <u>but</u> also hungry.   Subordinating

4. Underline the interjections in the following passage:

   Mary and Lisa were determined to surprise Staci on her birthday. " Oh Boy! She will never guess what we have planned," exclaimed Mary. Lisa, who seemed lost in thought, suddenly cried, "Hey! We forgot to order a cake." "Oh, No!," Mary gasped.

Answers: 1. a. between, bricks b. within, year c. beneath, window 2. a. True b. False c. False d. True e. False f. False g. False h. True 3. a. Coordinating b. Subordinating c. Correlative 4. Oh, Boy!, Hey!, Oh, No!

Chapter 6

PHRASES, CLAUSES, AND SENTENCES

Chapter Check-In

❑ Recognizing phrases

❑ Identifying independent and subordinate clauses

❑ Understanding sentences

Clauses and phrases are the building blocks of sentences. A phrase is a group of words that act as a part of speech but cannot stand alone as a sentence. Clauses are groups of words that have a subject and a predicate. Independent clauses express a complete thought and can stand alone as a sentence but subordinate clauses depend on other parts of the sentence to express a complete thought.

A sentence expresses a complete thought and contains a subject, a noun or pronoun, and a predicate, a verb or verb phrase. The four basic types of sentences—simple, compound, complex, and compound-complex—use phrases and clauses in varying degrees of complexity.

The Phrase

A **phrase** is any group of related words that, unlike a sentence, has no subject-predicate combination. The words in a phrase act together so that the phrase itself functions as a single part of speech. For example, some phrases act as nouns, some as verbs, some as adjectives or adverbs. Remember that phrases can't stand alone as sentences.

The chance that you'll ever be asked to differentiate between a gerund phrase and an infinitive phrase or a participial phrase and a prepositional phrase is small. So why learn about these phrases? First, if you understand how they work, you can avoid mistaking them for sentences. Second, you can avoid misplacing them or leaving them dangling in sentences (See

Chapter 7). Third, you can learn to use them effectively in combining sentences. A series of short, choppy sentences can be turned into a more mature, effective sentence by using phrases and clauses (See Chapter 6).

The Prepositional Phrase

The most common phrase is the **prepositional phrase.** You'll find these phrases everywhere—in sentences, clauses, and even in other phrases. Each prepositional phrase begins with a preposition *(in, of, by, from, for,* etc.; see Chapter 5 for a more complete list) and includes a noun or pronoun that is the object of the preposition.

> *in* the *room*
> *of* the *people*
> *by* the *river*
> *from* the *teacher*
> *for* the *party*

The object of a preposition can have its own modifiers, which also are part of the prepositional phrase.

> in *the smoky, crowded* room
> of *the remaining few* people
> by *the rushing* river
> from *the tired and frustrated* teacher
> for *the midnight victory* party

Prepositional phrases function as either adjectives or adverbs.

> The woman *in the trench coat* pulled out her cellular phone.

The prepositional phrase here acts as an adjective describing the noun *woman.*

> Most of the audience snoozed *during the tedious performance.*

The prepositional phrase here acts as an adverb modifying the verb *snoozed.*

Phrases Containing Verbals

To understand phrases containing gerunds, infinitives and participles see Chapter 2 for a complete review of **verbals.** Briefly, these verbals act as nouns, adjectives, and adverbs in sentences.

The participial phrase

A **participial phrase** begins with a past or present participle and is followed by its objects and modifiers. Like participles alone, participial phrases are used as adjectives.

> *Sniffing the fresh air,* Jim realized he had found paradise.

In the preceding sentence, the present participle *sniffing* introduces the participial phrase, which includes the participle's object *(air)* and its modifiers *(the, fresh)*. This participial phrase acts as an adjective modifying the subject of the sentence *(Jim)*.

> The soldiers, *trapped by the enemy,* threw down their guns.

Here, the past participle *trapped* introduces the participial phrase *trapped by the enemy.* The entire phrase acts as an adjective modifying the subject of the sentence *(soldiers)*. Notice the phrase-within-a-phrase here. By *the enemy* is a prepositional phrase modifying the participle *trapped.* Remember that phrases can act as modifiers in other phrases.

The gerund phrase

At first, a **gerund phrase** may look like a participial phrase because gerund phrases begin with the *-ing* form of a verb *(riding, seeing, talking,* etc.) and have objects and modifiers. But a gerund phrase always acts as a noun in a sentence, not as an adjective. Like other nouns, a gerund phrase can serve as the subject of a sentence, the object of a verb or preposition, or the complement of a linking verb.

In the following example, the gerund phrase *Riding the black stallion* acts as a noun and is the subject of the verb *terrified.*

> *Riding the black stallion* terrified Hugh.

In the next sentence, the gerund phrase *seeing the suspect* is the direct object of the verb reported. Notice that the entire phrase, not just the word *suspect,* is the direct object.

> The police officer reported *seeing the suspect.*

Here, the gerund phrase *talking often and loudly* is the object of the preposition *by.*

> The senator made his reputation by *talking often and loudly.*

In the final example, *Calling Uncle Roberto* is a gerund phrase acting as the subject of the sentence. *Asking for trouble* is a gerund phrase acting as a complement of the linking verb *is*.

Calling Uncle Roberto is *asking for trouble.*

The infinitive phrase

An **infinitive phrase** contains an infinitive (for example, *to sleep, to have slept, to consider, to throw*) and its objects and modifiers. Infinitive phrases usually function as nouns, though they can be used as adjectives and adverbs.

In this sentence, *To sleep all night* is an infinitive phrase acting as a noun. It is the subject of this sentence.

To sleep all night was his only wish.

Here, *To take an unpopular stand* is an infinitive phrase acting as a noun. It is the direct object of the predicate *didn't want.*

The representatives didn't want *to take an unpopular stand.*

Next, the infinitive phrase *to spend foolishly* acts as an adjective modifying the noun *money.*

He had plenty of money *to spend foolishly.*

In the following sentence, the infinitive phrase *to clear her mind* acts as an adverb modifying *drove.* It answers the question "Why did she drive?"

After the confrontation, she drove miles *to clear her mind.*

Split infinitives

Breaking up an infinitive with one or more adverbs is called **splitting an infinitive.** Splitting an infinitive isn't considered the grammatical sin it used to be, but most careful writers still don't split infinitives unless they have a reason to do so.

They taught her *to spend* money *wisely.*

NOT They taught her *to wisely spend* money.

Sometimes, however, not splitting an infinitive is almost impossible.

We expect the population *to more than double* over the next twenty years.

Other times, not splitting an infinitive causes ambiguity or sounds unnatural. In these cases, don't worry about breaking the old rule; clarity and smoothness take precedence over unsplit infinitives.

In this sentence, does *further* modify *Russian efforts* or *discuss?*

> We wanted *to discuss further Russian efforts* to modernize.

> Splitting the infinitive makes the sentence clearer.

> BETTER We wanted *to further discuss Russian efforts* to modernize.

> Splitting the infinitive in the following sentence makes it less stilted, more natural.

> He planned *to take quickly* the children to another room.

> BETTER He planned *to quickly take* the children to another room.

Types of Clauses

Like a phrase, a **clause** is a group of related words, but unlike a phrase, a clause has a subject and predicate. An **independent clause,** along with having a subject and predicate, expresses a complete thought and can stand alone as a sentence. On the contrary, a **subordinate** or **dependent clause** does not express a complete thought and therefore is *not* a sentence. A subordinate clause standing alone is the most common type of sentence fragment.

Independent clauses

He saw her; The Washingtons hurried home, Free speech has a price. Grammatically complete statements like these are sentences and can stand alone. When they are part of longer sentences, they are referred to as **independent** (or **main**) **clauses.**

Two or more independent clauses can be joined by using coordinating conjunctions *(and, but, for, nor, or, so,* and *yet)* or by using semicolons. The most important thing to remember is that an independent clause *can* stand alone as a complete sentence.

In the following example the independent clause is a simple sentence.

> *Erica brushed her long, raven hair.*

Here, the coordinating conjunction *and* joins two independent clauses:

> *Fernando left, and Erica brushed her long, raven hair.*

Here, a semicolon joins two independent clauses:

> *Fernando left; Erica brushed her long, raven hair.*

All sentences must include at least one independent clause.

> After she told Fernando to leave, *Erica brushed her long, raven hair.*

The independent clause is preceded by a clause that can't stand alone.

> *Erica brushed her long, raven hair* while she waited for Fernando to leave.

The independent clause is followed by a clause that can't stand alone.

Beginning sentences with coordinating conjunctions

Any of the coordinating conjunctions *(and, but, or, nor, for, so, yet)* can be used to join an independent clause to another independent clause. But can you *begin* a sentence with one of these conjunctions?

> No one knew what to do. *But* everyone agreed that something should be done.

An old rule says that you shouldn't. But beginning a sentence with a coordinating conjunction is widely accepted today. (Notice the preceding sentence, for example.) Sometimes beginning a sentence this way creates exactly the effect you want; it separates the clause and yet draws attention to its relationship with the previous clause. Use this technique when it works for you. If you're confronted with an advocate of the old rule, you'll have no trouble finding support for your position from the best writers and usage experts.

Subordinate clauses

A **subordinate clause** has a subject and predicate but, unlike an independent clause, cannot stand by itself. It *depends* on something else to express a complete thought, which is why it is also called a **dependent clause.** Some subordinate clauses are introduced by relative pronouns *(who, whom, that, which, what, whose)* and some by subordinating conjunctions *(although, because, if, unless, when,* etc.). Subordinate clauses function in sentences as adjectives, nouns, and adverbs.

Relative clauses

A **relative clause** begins with a relative pronoun and functions as an adjective.

In the following sentence, the relative pronoun *that* is the subject of its clause and *won* is the predicate. This clause couldn't stand by itself. Its role in the complete sentence is to modify *novel,* the subject of the independent clause.

> The novel *that won the Pulitzer Prize* didn't sell well when it was first published.

In the next example, *which* is the relative pronoun that begins the subordinate clause. *Celebrities* is the subject of the clause and *attended* is the predicate. In the complete sentence, this clause functions as an adjective describing *ceremony.*

> The ceremony, *which several celebrities attended,* received intense coverage.

Note that in a relative clause the relative pronoun is sometimes the subject of the clause, as in the following sentence, and sometimes the object, as in the next sentence.

> Arthur, *who comes to the games every week,* offered to be scorekeeper.

Who is the subject of the clause and *comes* is the predicate. The clause modifies *Arthur.*

In the following sentence, *mother* is the subject of the clause, *adored* is the predicate, and *whom* is the direct object of *adored.* Again, the clause modifies *Arthur.*

> Arthur, *whom* the team mother adored, was asked to be scorekeeper.

Noun clauses

A **noun clause** serves as a noun in a sentence.

> *What I want for dinner* is a hamburger. (subject of the predicate *is*)
> The host told us *how he escaped.* (object of the predicate *told*)
> The vacation is *what I need most.* (complement of the linking verb *is*)
> Give it to *whoever arrives first.* (object of the preposition *to*)

Pronoun case in subordinate clause

Who, whom, whoever, whomever. In deciding which case of *who* you should use in a clause, remember this important rule: The case of the pronoun is governed by the role it plays in its own clause, *not* by its relation to the rest of the sentence. Choosing the right case of pronoun can be especially confusing because the pronoun may appear to have more than one function. Look at the following sentence.

They gave the money to *whoever presented the winning ticket.*

At first, you may be tempted to think *whomever* rather than *whoever* should be the pronoun here, on the assumption that it is the object of the preposition *to*. But in fact the entire clause, not *whoever,* is the object of the preposition. Refer to the basic rule: The case should be based on the pronoun's role within its own clause. In this clause, *whoever* is the subject of the verb *presented.* (A good way to determine the right pronoun case is to forget everything but the clause itself: *whoever presented the winning ticket,* yes; *whomever presented the winning ticket,* no.)

The following two sentences show more dramatically how you must focus on the clause rather than the complete sentence in choosing the right pronoun case.

We asked *whomever we saw* for a reaction to the play.

We asked *whoever called* us to call back later.

In each sentence the clause is the direct object of asked. But in the first sentence, *whomever* is correct because within its clause it is the object of saw, while in the second sentence, *whoever* is correct because it is the subject of *called.*

Adverbial clauses

Many subordinate clauses begin with subordinating conjunctions called **adverbial clauses**. Examples of these conjunctions are *because, unless, if, when,* and *although.* For a more complete list, see Chapter 5. What these conjunctions have in common is that they make the clauses that follow them unable to stand alone. The clauses act as adverbs, answering questions like *how, when, where, why, to what extent,* and *under what conditions.*

> *While Mauna Loa was erupting and spewing fountains of lava into the air,* we drove away as quickly as we could.

In the preceding sentence, *while* is a subordinating conjunction introducing the adverbial clause; the subject of the clause is *Mauna Loa* and the predicate is *was erupting* and *[was] spewing.* This clause is dependent because it is an incomplete thought. What *happened* while the volcano was erupting? The independent clause *we drove away as quickly as we could* completes the thought. The adverbial clause answers the question "When did we drive?"

In the following sentence, *because* introduces the adverbial clause in which *van* is the subject and *needed* the predicate. This clause is an incomplete thought. What *happened* because the van needed repairs? The independent clause *The group of tourists decided to have lunch in the village* is necessary to complete the thought. Again, the subordinate clause as a whole acts as an adverb, telling why the tourists decided to have lunch in the village.

> The group of tourists decided to have lunch in the village *because the van needed repairs.*

The Sentence

The standard definition of a **sentence** is that it is a group of words containing a subject and a predicate and expressing a complete thought. But for this definition to be helpful, you must be able to recognize a subject and a predicate and understand what is meant by "a complete thought."

Subject and predicate

A sentence has a **subject** (what or whom the sentence is about) and a predicate. The **predicate** tells what the subject does or is or what is done to the subject (for example, The books *were left* outside). The **simple subject** is a noun or pronoun. The **complete subject** is this noun or pronoun and the words that modify it. The **simple predicate** is a verb or verb phrase (for example, *has walked, will have walked*). The **complete predicate** is the verb or verb phrase and the words that modify or complete it.

In this example, *Fred* is both the simple and the complete subject of the sentence. *Shot* is the simple predicate. *Shot Guido* is the complete predicate: the verb *shot* and its direct object *Guido*. (For direct object, see Chapter 2.)

> *Fred shot Guido.*

In the following example, *man* is the simple subject. *The angry old man in pajamas* is the complete subject. *Stood* is the verb; *stood on the porch* is the complete predicate.

> *The angry old man in pajamas stood on the porch.*

In this sentence, *The argument that money is a burden* is the complete subject. *Argument* is the simple subject modified by the adjective clause *that money is a burden*. The rest of the sentence is complete predicate. The simple predicate is the verb *originated*.

> *The argument that money is a burden probably originated with a rich man who was trying to counter the envy of a poor man.*

In the first sentence, subject and predicate are easy to identify. In the second sentence, you can still pick out the simple subject and verb fairly easily, despite the modifiers. But the third sentence is more complicated. As you begin to write more sophisticated sentences, the simple subject and simple predicate may seem to get lost in a web of modifying words, phrases, and clauses. To ensure that you have a complete sentence, however, you still should be able to identify the core noun or pronoun and the core verb or verb phrase.

Expressing a complete thought

In addition to having a subject and predicate, a sentence must be able to stand on its own. It can't depend on something else to express a complete thought. Look at the following examples.

> *He jumped.*

This is a grammatically complete sentence, though perhaps not an interesting one. It has a subject *(he)* and a predicate *(jumped).* It expresses a complete thought—you know what happened. You might want to know more about the person—who he is or why he jumped, for example. You might want to know more about the jump itself—when it occurred, how high it was, and so on. But the basic action is complete: *He jumped.*

The next example is an incomplete sentence. It still has a subject *(he)* and a predicate *(jumped),* but the presence of *When* keeps this group of words from being a complete thought: What *happened* when he jumped?

> *When he jumped.*

The following sentence is still an incomplete sentence. Now, you know something about where he jumped, but the thought is still incomplete: What *happened* when he jumped high into the air?

> *When he jumped high into the air.*

The next example is a complete sentence again. The question "What happened when he jumped?" has been answered: *he looked as if he were flying.* Even if the phrase *high into the air* were to be deleted, the thought would be complete.

> *When he jumped high into the air, he looked as if he were flying.*

Sentence Types: Simple, Compound, and Complex

Your ability to vary sentence types in your writing will allow you to control the pacing and clarity of your paragraphs. Using a variety of sentence types also makes for more interesting reading.

A **simple sentence** has one independent clause and no subordinate clauses.

Old-growth forests in the United States are disappearing.
Citizens must act.

A **compound sentence** has two or more independent clauses, joined by coordinating conjunctions, and no subordinate clauses.

Old-growth forests in the United States are disappearing, and citizens must act. (two independent clauses joined by *and*)

A **complex sentence** contains one independent clause and one or more subordinate clauses.

Because old growth forests in the United States are fast disappearing, citizens must act now. (*Because old growth forests in the United States are fast disappearing* = subordinate clause beginning with subordinating conjunction; *citizens must act now* = independent clause)

Forests that have existed for thousands of years are in danger. (*that have existed for thousands of years* = subordinate clause beginning with relative pronoun; *Forests . . . are in danger* = independent clause)

A **compound-complex sentence** joins two or more independent clauses with one or more subordinate clauses.

Forests that have existed for thousands of years are in danger, and citizens must take action. (*Forests are in danger* and *citizens must take action* = independent clauses; *that have existed for thousands of years* = subordinate clause)

Make use of all these types of sentences. Don't string together a long series of simple sentences, but, on the other hand, don't always write compound and complex sentences. Try beginning with a simple sentence, or try following several long compound and complex sentences with a simple one. It can have a surprisingly forceful effect.

Because America seemed to provide limitless natural resources, until the second half of this century we spent them freely. We mined for minerals, diverted rivers, and cut down trees, many of which had been growing for thousands of years before the first settlers arrived. Over the years, America's wilderness has given way to prosperous cities, and skyscrapers have replaced giant old trees. *America has succeeded. But now we are paying the price.*

Chapter Checkout

Q&A

1. Identify the following underlined phrases as prepositional phrase, participial phrase, gerund phrase, or infinitive phrase.

    a. <u>Dreaming about mice</u> is my cat Mocha's favorite hobby.

    b. Kevin wants <u>to make</u> the world a better place.

    c. <u>Lying on his bed</u>, Richard felt better.

    d. Ted sneezed <u>in church.</u>

    e. Dr. Tucker planned <u>to have read</u> that book.

2. Identify the function of the underlined dependent clauses.

    a. <u>When my father called from Israel</u>, Mother threw down her knitting and hurried to answer the phone.

    b. The prom, <u>which is usually held in May</u>, was delayed by the late snowstorm.

    c. <u>Whoever adjusted my seat</u> must have been tall.

3. True or False: All of the following are independent clauses.

    a. Sherry smiled.

    b. The Russian impressionist collection, with all their dramatic colors and themes.

    c. To have been loved is to have known joy and pain

4. Underline the complete subject in the following sentences.

    a. My cousin Andy, a shy man, was married last summer.

    b. The office will be closed on Thursday.

    c. Get ready!

5. Underline the complete predicate in the following sentences.

    a. Through the quiet, dark streets came Lizz, determined not to get lost.

    b. After a deep winter sleep, the bears emerged hesitantly.

    c. Andrei visited the Grand Canyon last summer.

Answers: 1. a. gerund b. infinitive c. participial d. prepositional e. infinitive. 2. a. Adverb b. Adjective c. Noun. 3. a. True b. False c. True. 4. a. My cousin Andy, a shy young man b. The office c. You (implied subject). 5. a. Through the quiet, dark streets came, determined not to get lost b. After a deep winter sleep, emerged hesitantly c. visited the Grand Canyon last summer.

Chapter 7

COMMON SENTENCE ERRORS

Chapter Check-In

- ❑ Avoiding run-on sentences
- ❑ Identifying and correcting sentence fragments
- ❑ Checking subject-predicate agreement
- ❑ Preventing misplaced modifiers
- ❑ Following parallel structure

Once you understand what a sentence is, you'll be able to tell what works and what doesn't work. To avoid errors like run-on sentences and fragments, you should learn to recognize how complete sentences are put together. Other errors, such as lack of subject-predicate agreement, misplaced modifiers, faulty parallelism, and style problems like wordiness, require careful attention to the way words function within a sentence. As a critical reviewer of your own writing, you'll be able to avoid these mistakes.

Run-On Sentences

One of the most common mistakes with independent clauses is joining them without the proper punctuation. This error is called a **run-on sentence** or **comma splice.** An independent clause standing alone should end in a period, question mark, or exclamation point.

Joining independent clauses

If you want to join independent clauses, however, you should use a semi-colon or one of the seven coordinating conjunctions between them (see Chapter 5). A comma should precede the coordinating conjunction, but a comma without a conjunction is not sufficient.

He drove off in the *Mercedes, Erica* watched him go. (no)

This is a run-on sentence, or comma splice. A comma alone cannot join independent clauses.

He drove off in the *Mercedes. Erica* watched him go. (yes)

Here, the independent clauses are separate sentences. Each ends correctly with a period.

He drove off in the *Mercedes; Erica* watched him go. (yes)

The two independent clauses are correctly joined with a semicolon.

He drove off in the *Mercedes, and* Erica watched him go. (yes)

The two independent clauses are correctly joined with a coordinating conjunction *(and)* preceded by a comma.

Run-ons with conjunctive (sentence) adverbs

Watch out for another kind of run-on sentence. Some words look like coordinating conjunctions but aren't. These words *cannot* be used to join independent clauses with a comma. Remember that the only time you can join independent clauses with a comma and not be guilty of a run-on sentence is when one of the seven coordinating conjunctions *(and, but, for, nor, or, so, yet)* follows the comma.

The impostors—words that look suspiciously like coordinating conjunctions but are actually adverbs—we called conjunctive adverbs or sentence adverbs. The use of a comma to join a clause beginning with one of these words is widespread in business and official writing, but no matter how common the practice, it still creates a run-on, and most teachers and editors won't accept it. Table 7-1 shows a few of the words to watch out for.

Table 7-1   Conjunctive Adverbs

also	moreover
besides	nevertheless
consequently	otherwise
further, furthermore	similarly
hence	then
however	therefore
indeed	thus
likewise	

Some transitional phrases pose the same problem—for example, *as a result, even so, for example, in other words, on the contrary.* If you keep in mind the rule that independent clauses can be joined with a comma only when the comma is followed by one of the seven coordinating conjunctions, you should be able to avoid these tricky run-ons.

> Scientists were convinced by the *evidence; however,* the Food and Drug Administration was slow to respond.

> NOT   Scientists were convinced by the *evidence, however,* the Food and Drug Administration was slow to respond.

> The hurricane damaged the *arena. Nevertheless,* the game was played on schedule.

> NOT   The hurricane damaged the *arena, nevertheless,* the game was played on schedule.

> Folic acid appears to exert a protective *effect. For example,* one study showed that it cut the rate of neural tube defects by two-thirds.

> NOT   Folic acid appears to exert a protective *effect, for example,* one study showed that it cut the rate of neural tube defects by two-thirds.

Acceptable run-ons

Run-on sentences such as the ones described above are basic errors. Occasionally, however, joining independent clauses with only a comma may be acceptable—for example, when the clauses are very short and have the same form, when the tone is easy and conversational, or when you feel that the rhythm of your sentence calls for it.

> *Live by the sword, die by the sword.*
> *They smiled, they touched, they kissed.*
> *I hardly recognized her, she was so thin.* (A *because* is understood here.)

But be very careful about creating an intentional run-on. Have a good reason to do so; don't break such a basic sentence rule lightly.

Sentence Fragments

Most **sentence fragments** are phrases, or subordinate clauses, or combinations of the two. Don't ever let length be your guide, for a sentence can be two words *(He jumps)* and a fragment fifty.

Recognizing fragments

At first glance, a sentence fragment may look like a sentence because it begins with a capital letter and ends with a period. When you look more closely, however, you'll see that the group of words is missing one or more of the three elements required to make it a sentence: a subject, a predicate, and a grammatically complete thought.

> *Unless you want more coverage than the newspaper story.* (fragment)

This is a subordinate clause. It is missing an independent clause that would complete the thought.

> Unless you want more coverage than the newspaper story, *we have made all the arrangements.* (sentence)

When you write sentences beginning with subordinating conjunctions, make sure that you have an independent clause following the subordinate clause.

> We saw the boys standing there. *Laughing and throwing cans all over the front lawn.* (fragment)

A sentence here is followed by a fragment, a participial phrase that cannot stand alone. The problem could be solved if the period after *there* were changed to a comma.

> He pointed at Mrs. Wolfe. *The woman who wore the hard hat and the tool belt.* (fragment)

The pronoun *who* makes this a relative clause that can't stand alone. It acts as an appositive (see Chapter 3) identifying Mrs. Wolfe, and it should be joined to the main clause with a comma.

> *The chairman of the committee, whose term was dependent on his party's being in power, which was, according to most of the polls, unlikely to be the case after the next general election.* (fragment)

This is a more complicated fragment, consisting of a subject and two subordinate clauses, each containing phrases. You don't need to identify all the elements in this fragment, but realize that a predicate for the subject of the sentence *(chairman)* is missing. To make a complete sentence, add a predicate, for example, *insisted on bringing the motion to a vote.*

The last example is typical of the sophisticated fragments that might escape your notice. Keep your eye on the three key requirements: subject, predicate, complete thought. It's particularly important to check a complicated sentence you've written just to make sure it isn't a complicated fragment instead.

Acceptable fragments

Some sentence fragments are acceptable, although a teacher may prefer that you avoid all of them while learning to write. Intentional fragments can be found throughout good writing.

In dialogue, to use an obvious example, fragments are appropriately conversational.

> "Where are you going?" I asked.
>
> *"Out for a walk."* She glowered at me.

Experienced writers also use fragments occasionally to create a particular effect, make a point emphatically, or answer a question they've asked:

> Many of the people who drove by refused to stop and help. *But not all of them.*
>
> Scorcese had offered me a bit part in the movie. *The chance of a lifetime!* And she wanted me to turn it down.
>
> Why should you consider a two-year rather than a four-year college? *For many reasons.*

Before you consider using an intentional fragment, be sure you understand correct sentence structure, as an unintentional fragment is a glaring error. Also, be sure using a fragment is warranted: Could you achieve the effect you're after without it? In the second example above, a dash after *movie* would achieve the same effect that the fragment does.

> Scorcese had offered me a bit part in the movie—*the chance of a lifetime!*

Subject–Predicate Agreement

Noun-verb agreement is discussed in Chapter 1. Which verb to choose for particular pronouns (for example, *everyone, each, anyone*) is discussed in Chapter 3. But to make sure that you don't have subject-predicate agreement problems in a complete sentence, you must know more than that the noun *team* usually takes a singular verb, that the noun *criteria* takes a plural verb, or that *everyone, each,* and *anyone* take singular verbs. Within a sentence are distractions that can make you misidentify subject and predicate, leading to an agreement problem. Remember that a predicate (verb) must agree in person and number with its subject, regardless of other elements in a sentence.

Locating the subject

Your first job is to locate the subject of the sentence. To do this, find the verb, the action word or the state-of-being word, and then determine who or what is being talked about. Then ask yourself, "Is the subject first, second, or third person *(I/we; you; he, she, it/they)*? Is the subject singular or plural?" When you've answered these questions, you will know which form the verb should take. Singular subjects take singular verbs, and plural subjects take plural verbs.

Subject–predicate agreement with a compound subject

In sentences with more than one subject, the word *and* usually appears between the elements.

Use a plural verb with a compound subject.

> *Drinking* a glass of milk *and soaking* in the tub *help* me fall asleep.
>
> NOT *Drinking* a glass of milk *and soaking* in the tub *helps* me fall asleep.
>
> A concerned *teacher and* a vigilant *parent urge* her to take the exam.
>
> NOT A concerned *teacher and* a vigilant *parent urges* her to take the exam.

If *each* or *every* precedes a compound subject, however, treat the subject as singular.

> *Each dog and cat is* to be fed twice a day.
>
> *Every house and garage has* been searched.

Additive phrases

An **additive phrase** sometimes makes a sentence look as *if* it has a compound subject. Examples of these phrases are *accompanied by, along with, as well as, in addition to, including, and together with.* When you use one of them, you are thinking of more than one person or thing. But grammatically these phrases aren't conjunctions like *and.* They are actually modifying the subject, not making it compound. Therefore, do not choose a plural verb because of one of these modifying phrases.

> President *Ford, accompanied by* his advisors, *was* en route to Europe.
>
> NOT President *Ford, accompanied by* his advisors, *were* en route to Europe.
>
> The *instructor, along with* the class, *is* angry about the room change.

NOT   The *instructor, along with* the class, *are* angry about the room change.

Phrases and clauses between subject and predicate

Watch out for phrases and clauses that come between the subject and predicate of your sentence. Such interruptions can throw you off. To make sure you have the right person and number for the verb, mentally eliminate intervening phrases and clauses.

> The *speech* that provoked the subsequent activities and caused the closing of the university *was filled* with inaccuracies.

NOT   The *speech* that provoked the subsequent activities and caused the closing of the university *were filled* with inaccuracies.

Find the predicate *(was/were filled)* and ask yourself, "What was filled with inaccuracies?" This question will help you locate the subject *(speech).* By eliminating the intervening clauses, you have *speech was filled.*

Subject following predicate

Although the standard word order in an English sentence is subject-verb-object, exceptions abound.

Don't count on word order in identifying your subject.

> Off in the comer, out of plain sight, *sits* the famous *artist.* (predicate-subject)

If you decide to put a subject after a verb, be sure to check agreement.

> In the doorway *wait* the *head of the mob and two of his thugs.*

NOT   In the doorway *waits* the *head of the mob and two of his thugs.*

Because the subject is compound, you need the plural form of the verb.

In the construction *there is* or *there are, there* is never the subject. Because these constructions tend to be dead weight, it is best to limit them (See Chapter 11). If you do use a *there is* or a *there are,* however, remember that your subject will follow the predicate. Choose is if the subject is singular, are if the subject is plural.

> *There are millions* of people who would rather be poor than ask for government help.

NOT   *There is* (or *There's*) millions of people who would rather be poor than ask for government help.

(But why not *Millions of people would rather be poor than ask for government help?*)

Subject–predicate agreement

The conjunctions *or, either . . . or,* and *neither . . . nor* ask you to choose between things rather than add things (unlike *and 16*). If both elements are singular, use a singular verb. If both elements are plural, use a plural verb. If one element is singular and one is plural, choose the verb to agree with the element closest to it.

> The *director or* the *assistant director is* planning to be on location.
>
> NOT The *director or* the *assistant director are* planning to be on location.

In the previous examples, both elements are singular and therefore the verb is singular. In the following example, one element *(coach)* is singular and one *(members)* is plural. Since the plural is closer to the verb, the verb should be plural *(were)*.

> *Either* the *coach or* the *team members were* responsible for the dispute.
>
> NOT *Either* the *coach or* the *team members was* responsible for the dispute.

It is better when using a subject with one singular and one plural element to put the plural closest to the verb or to rewrite the sentence entirely to avoid awkwardness.

Subject–predicate agreement in relative clauses

Agreement problems can occur in relative clauses using *which, that,* or, *one of those who.*

The verb in a relative clause must agree with the relative pronoun's antecedent (the word the pronoun stands for). Always ask yourself what the relative pronoun refers to.

> He decided to write *novels, which are* his favorite form.
>
> NOT He decided to write *novels, which is* his favorite form.

Novels is the antecedent of *which,* and therefore the verb must be plural *(are)*. A common mistake is to choose the verb that agrees with the complement in the relative clause *(form)*. Remember that the complement is not the antecedent of the pronoun.

The construction *one of those who* causes confusion when it comes to subject-verb agreement in the relative clause. Decide whether *one* or *those* is the antecedent of *who* in choosing the right verb.

In the following sentence, the antecedent is *bosses,* and therefore the plural *verb believe* is correct.

Connie is *one of those bosses who believe* in giving their employees freedom to make decisions.

The addition of *only* makes it clear that the antecedent is *one* rather than *bosses,* and therefore the singular verb *believes* is appropriate.

Connie is the *only one of the bosses who believes* in giving her employees freedom to make decisions.

When you use a *one of those who* construction, look at the clause beginning with *who* and then decide what the antecedent is. In most cases you will decide on the plural form of the verb.

Dr. Wolfe is *one of those teachers who entertain* students as well as teach them.

One of those business owners who believe in putting the customer first, Jim won the loyalty of the community.

Note that while the *case of the pronoun* (*who* or *whom*) depends on the pronoun's role in its own clause (see Chapter 6), the *number of the verb* depends on the pronoun's antecedent.

Placement of Modifiers

Keep related parts of a sentence together to avoid the common mistake of a misplaced modifier. If it isn't clear in a sentence exactly which term a modifier applies to, it is a **misplaced modifier**.

Misplaced modifiers

Any kind of modifier can be misplaced: an adjective, an adverb, a phrase or clause acting as an adjective or adverb. If you put a modifier in a place it doesn't belong, you risk confusion, awkwardness, and even unintentional humor.

He saw *a truck in the driveway that was red and black.* (misplaced modifier)

If red and black are the colors of the truck rather than the driveway, write the sentence so that this is clear.

He saw *a red and black truck* in the driveway.

In the next sentence, it's doubtful that Anna wanted to be cremated before she died, but the placement of the adverbial phrase suggests that's just what she wanted.

Perhaps anticipating what modern science would discover, Anna Anderson, who claimed to be the missing Anastasia, requested she be cremated *before her death.* (misplaced modifier)

Rewrite the sentence to make it clear that the phrase *before her death* modifies *requested,* not *cremated.*

Perhaps anticipating what modern science would discover, Anna Anderson, who claimed to be the missing Anastasia, *requested before her death* that she be cremated.

In the following sentence, the placement of the modifier *by Friday* leaves us with a question: Did we know by Friday, or would we call for a strike by Friday?

We knew *by Friday* we would call for a strike. (unclear modifier)

To avoid any possible confusion, add *that.*

> *We knew that by Friday we would call for a strike.*
> OR *We knew by Friday that we would call for a strike.* (depending on your meaning)

In these examples, the suggested rewritten versions are not the only possible ways to correct the problem. Play around with your own sentences when you find confusing modifiers; you may not only correct the problem but also improve the sentence by making it more concise or changing its emphasis.

Remember that the placement of even a simple modifier can change the meaning of a sentence. Watch the effect of the placement of *not* below.

Not all the home-team players were available.

All the home-team players were *not available.*

In the first sentence, maybe the home team could still limp along through a game. In the second, the game would definitely be canceled.

Misplaced participial phrases

Among the most common misplaced modifiers are participial phrases. Beginning writers often overlook whether the subject of the participial phrase is clear to the reader.

Advancing across the desolate plains, the hot sun burned the *pioneers.* (misplaced modifier)

If not the sun but the pioneers are advancing, make this clear.

> *Advancing across the desolate plains, the pioneers* were burned by the hot sun.

OR   *The hot sun burned the pioneers advancing across the desolate plains.* (if you want to avoid the passive voice)

No matter how you decide to rewrite the sentence, you must make sure the modifier is modifying the right word.

In the following example, the placement of *on the hillside* between *buildings* and the participial phrase *constructed of highly flammable materials* doesn't cause serious confusion; we probably realize that it is the buildings that are constructed of highly flammable materials, not the hillside.

> The *buildings on the hillside constructed of highly flammable materials* were destroyed first. (misplaced modifier)

But improve the sentence by placing the modifier next to the word that it modifies:

> *On the hillside, the buildings constructed of highly flammable materials were destroyed first.*

In the next example, the question is: In his glass case, was the collector preserving the ancient woman or only her teeth?

> The *teeth of the ancient woman preserved in a glass case* were the pride of his collection. (unclear modifier)

If the answer is her teeth, then rewrite the sentence to better place the participial phrase *preserved in a glass case*.

> The ancient woman's *teeth, preserved in a glass case,* were the pride of his collection,

OR   *Preserved in a glass case, the teeth* of the ancient woman were the pride of his collection.

Dangling modifiers

Dangling modifiers are similar to misplaced modifiers except that the modifier isn't just separated from the word it modifies; it is *missing* the word it modifies. The writer has the term being modified in mind—but not on paper.

> *Having eaten dinner,* the idea of a cheeseburger was unappealing. (dangling modifier)

The dangling participle is the most notorious of the dangling modifiers. In this example, the participial phrase *Having eaten dinner* has nothing to modify; it certainly is not modifying *idea* or *cheeseburger.* One way to correct the problem is simply to add the missing word.

> *Having eaten dinner, I found the idea of a cheeseburger unappealing.*

In the following example, the participial phrase *Studying the lecture notes* dangles in this sentence.

> *Studying the lecture notes,* the ecosystem became clear. (dangling modifier)

It doesn't modify *ecosystem.* Rewrite the sentence.

> *The ecosystem became clear when I studied the lecture notes.*

In the next sentence, the infinitive phrase *To win the election* is lacking a word to modify; it cannot modify *money.*

> *To win the election, money* is essential. (dangling modifier)

Rewrite the sentence to add an appropriate subject.

> *To win the election, a candidate needs money.*

In the following sentence, *When upset and sad* is an **elliptical clause,** meaning that a word or words have been omitted. In this clause, a subject and verb are missing; they are implied but not stated: *When (she was) upset and sad.*

> *When upset and sad, her room* was her refuge. (dangling modifier)

Elliptical clauses are acceptable, but a subject must follow one or the clause will dangle.

> *When upset and sad, she used her room as a refuge.*

Parallel Structure

Parallelism in sentences refers to matching grammatical structures. Elements in a sentence that have the same function or express similar ideas should be grammatically parallel, or grammatically matched. Parallelism is used effectively as a rhetorical device throughout literature and in speeches, advertising copy, and popular songs.

> I sighed as a lover, I obeyed as a son.—Edward Gibbon
>
> Reading is to the mind what exercise is to the body.—Joseph Addison
>
> Blessed is the man that walketh not in the counsel of the ungodly, nor standeth in the way of sinners, nor sittith in the seat of the scornful.—The Book of Psalms 1:1

> Ask not what your country can do for you; ask what you can do for your country.—John F. Kennedy

Parallelism lends balance and grace to writing. It can make a sentence memorable. But even in prose not destined for greatness, parallelism is important.

Faulty parallelism

A failure to create grammatically parallel structures when they are appropriate is referred to as **faulty parallelism.** Notice the difference between correct parallel structure and faulty parallelism.

> What counts isn't *how you look* but *how you behave.*
>
> NOT What counts isn't *how you look* but *your behavior.*

> The president promises to *reform* health care, *preserve* social security, and *balance* the budget.
>
> NOT The president promises to *reform* health care, *preserve* social security, and *a balanced budget.*

Check for faulty parallelism in your own writing. Nouns should be parallel with nouns, participles with participles, gerunds with gerunds, infinitives with infinitives, clauses with clauses, and so on. Be particularly vigilant in the following situations.

Parallel structure in a series

When your sentence includes a series, make sure you have not used different grammatical structures for the items.

> He described *skiing* in the Alps, *swimming* in the Adriatic, and *the drive* across the Sahara Desert. (faulty parallelism)

> He described *skiing* in the Alps, *swimming* in the Adriatic, and *driving* across the Sahara Desert. (parallel)

In the parallel version, all the elements in the series begin with gerunds: *skiing, swimming, driving.* In the nonparallel version, the final element is a noun but not a gerund.

The elements would remain parallel in the correct version even if the phrases following the gerunds were changed or omitted. The length of the items in the series does not affect the parallel structure.

> He described *skiing, swimming* in the Adriatic, and *driving* across the desert. (parallel)

It doesn't matter what grammatical structure you choose for your series as long as you remain with it consistently.

> Eleanor liked to *have* a beer, *exchange* stories with her pals, and *watch* the men walk by. (parallel)

> Eleanor liked *having* a beer, *exchanging* stories with her pals, and *watching* the men walk by. (parallel)

When you use words such as *to, a, an, his, her,* or *their* with items in a series, you can use the word with the first item, thus having it apply to all the items, or you can repeat it with each item. However, if you repeat it, you must do so with all the items, not just some of them.

> Eleanor liked *to have* a beer, *to exchange* stories with her pals, and *to watch* the men walk by. (parallel)

> Eleanor liked *to have* a beer, *exchange* stories with her pals, and *to watch* the men walk by. (not parallel)

> He liked *their* courage, stamina, and style. (parallel)

> He liked *their* courage, *their* stamina, and *their* style. (parallel)

> He liked *their* courage, stamina, and *their* style. (not parallel)

> She saw *a* van, car, and pick-up collide. (parallel)

> She saw *a* van, *a* car, and *a* pick-up collide. (parallel)

> She saw *a* van, *a* car, and pick-up collide. (not parallel)

Parallel structure in comparisons and antithetical constructions

When you are comparing things in a sentence, obviously parallelism will be important. Make sure that the elements you are comparing or contrasting are grammatically parallel:

> He spoke more *of being ambassador* than *of being president.*

> NOT He spoke more *of his term as ambassador* than *being* president.

> *The schools in the suburbs* are better than *the schools in the inner city.*

> NOT *The schools in the suburbs* are better than *the inner city.*

In the second sentence, *schools* are being contrasted to the *inner city.* What the writer wants to contrast are schools in the suburbs with schools in the inner city.

In antithetical constructions, something is true of one thing but not another. *But not* and *rather than are* used to set up these constructions, and, as with comparisons, both parts of an antithetical construction should be parallel.

> The administration approved the student's right *to drop* the class but not *to meet* with the professor.
>
> NOT The administration approved the student's right *to drop* the class but not *meeting* with the professor.
>
> The committee chose *to table* the motion rather than *to vote* on it.
>
> NOT The committee chose *to table* the motion rather than *voting* on it.

Parallel structure with correlative conjunctions

Errors in parallel structure often occur with correlative conjunctions: *either . . . or; neither . . . nor; both . . . and; not only . . . but also; whether . . . or.* The grammatical structure following the second half of the correlative should mirror the grammatical structure following the first half.

> The scientists disputed <u>not only</u> *the newspaper article* <u>but also</u> *the university's official statement.* (parallel: phrase with phrase)
>
> The scientists disputed <u>not only</u> *the newspaper article* <u>but also</u> *they disputed the university's official statement.* (faulty parallelism: phrase with clause)
>
> <u>Either</u> *I like the job* <u>or</u> *I don't like it.* (parallel: clause matched with clause)
>
> <u>Either</u> *I like the job* <u>or</u> *I don't.* (parallel: clause matched with clause)
>
> <u>Either</u> *I like the job* <u>or</u> *not.* (faulty parallelism: clause matched with adverb)
>
> I have <u>neither</u> *the patience to complete it* <u>nor</u> *the desire to complete it.* (parallel: noun phrase with noun phrase)
>
> I have <u>neither</u> *the patience to complete it* <u>nor</u> *do I desire to complete it.* (faulty parallelism: phrase matched with clause)

You can improve this sentence even more:

> I have <u>neither</u> *the patience* <u>nor</u> *the desire* to complete it.

Patience and *desire* are both nouns, and the phrase *to complete it* can serve both of them.

Be sure that any element you want to repeat appears *after* the first half of the correlative conjunction. Look at the position of *as* in the following examples. In the second sentence, *as* appears before *either* and is repeated after *or,* which makes the construction not parallel.

> They acted *either as* individual citizens *or as* members of the committee,

NOT They acted *as either* individual citizens *or as* members of the committee.

In the following example, the last sentence, *we expected* appears *before* the first half of the correlative conjunction and should not be repeated after the second half.

> We expected <u>not only</u> to be late <u>but also</u> to be exhausted.

OR *We expected to be* <u>not only</u> late <u>but also</u> exhausted. (better)

BUT NOT *We expected* <u>not only</u> to be late <u>but also</u> *we expected* to be exhausted.

Parallel structure with verbs

When you have more than one verb in a sentence, be sure to make the verbs parallel by not shifting tenses unnecessarily (See Chapter 3). Also, don't shift from an active to a passive verb.

> Kate *prepared* the speech on the plane and *delivered* it at the conference. (parallel: both verbs are active)

> Kate *prepared* the speech on the plane, and it *was delivered* by her at the conference. (faulty parallelism: active and passive verb)

Sometimes sentences use a single verb form with two helping verbs. Look at the following example.

> We *can,* and I promise we *will, ensure* that this does not occur. (correct)

This sentence is correct because both *can* and *will* are correct with the base verb *ensure.* But look at this example.

> Robert *has* in the past and *will* in the future *continue to support* the measure. (incorrect)

To support belongs with *will continue,* but not with *has.* If you read the sentence without *and will in the future continue,* you will see this immediately: *Robert has in the past to support the measure.* Rewrite the sentence to include a participial form for *has.*

> Robert *has* in the past *supported,* and *will* in the future *continue to support,* the measure.

OR Just as Robert *has supported* this measure in the past, he *will continue to support* it in the future.

When writing paragraphs, vary your sentences in type and length. Either a series of choppy sentences or a string of long sentences can bore or frustrate a reader. Experiment too with different word order within your sentences.

Combining Sentences

Writers, particularly inexperienced ones, sometimes create a series of short sentences that sound choppy and lack good connections. If you can vary the length and complexity of your sentences, you will increase your reader's interest in your ideas.

Combining simple sentences

If you have written a series of simple sentences, try alternate methods of combining them to vary the pacing of the paragraph.

Look at the following example.

> Old-growth forests are disappearing. Citizens should take action. For example, wood substitutes are becoming more available. People can ask their contractors to use these substitutes.

These simple sentences can be combined to make compound and complex sentences.

> Old-growth forests are disappearing, and citizens should take action. For example, people can ask their contractors to use wood substitutes, which are becoming more available.

Be sure when you combine simple sentences that you let meaning be your guide. For example, use a complex sentence if you want to make one idea subordinate to another and a compound sentence if you want to join ideas of equal weight. In the example above, the first two clauses are of equal weight: the forests are disappearing, and people should do something about it. In the second sentence, the main idea is that people should ask their contractors to use wood substitutes; the subordinate point is that these substitutes are becoming more available.

Review coordinating conjunctions, subordinating conjunctions (Chapter 5) and conjunctive adverbs (Chapter 7), to see the relationships you can show when combining sentences.

Combining sentences using phrases

You can combine short sentences by using phrases as well as clauses. (Review different types of phrases in Chapter 6.) Look at the following example.

Scientists first identify the defective gene. Then they can create a screening test. Physicians can use this screening test to diagnose the condition early.

BETTER   After identifying the defective gene, scientists can develop a screening test to help physicians diagnose the condition early.

Notice that in the second version the participial phrase *After identifying the defective gene* and the infinitive phrase *to help physicians diagnose the condition early,* turn three choppy sentences into one smooth one.

Varying Word Order in Sentences

Instead of beginning every sentence with the simple subject, try beginning with a modifier, an appositive, or the main verb. You can also try delaying completion of your main statement or interrupting sentences with parenthetical elements. Look at the following examples.

Begin with a single-word modifier.

Suddenly the wind rushed into the room.

INSTEAD OF   The wind *suddenly* rushed into the room.

Begin with a modifying phrase or clause.

Unregulated and easily accessible, the Internet is a powerful force.

INSTEAD OF   The Internet, *unregulated and easily accessible,* is a powerful force.

In front of an audience, she was a star.

INSTEAD OF   She was a star *in front of an audience.*

When the manager told me what the apartment cost, I decided living at home with Mom and Dad wasn't so bad.

INSTEAD OF   I decided living at home with Mom and Dad wasn't so bad *when the manager told me what the apartment cost.*

Begin with an appositive (See Chapter 3).

A frequently misdiagnosed condition, iron overload can lead to serious diseases.

INSTEAD OF   Iron overload, *a frequently misdiagnosed condition,* can lead to serious diseases.

Put the verb before the subject

> Directly in front of him *stood his father*
>
> INSTEAD OF *His father stood* directly in front of him.

> Greater than the novel's shortcomings *are its strengths.*
>
> INSTEAD OF *The novel's strengths* are greater than its shortcomings.

Delay completing your main statement.

> *We saw the ballot measure,* so important to the students, the faculty, and indeed everyone in the community, *lose by a one-percent margin.*
>
> INSTEAD OF *We saw the ballot measure lose by a one-percent margin* even though it was so important to the students, the faculty, and indeed everyone in the community.

Insert an interruption—a surprise element—in a sentence; use parentheses or dashes.

> My home town—*it is closer to being a junction than a town*—recently acquired its first traffic light.

Never sacrifice meaning or clarity for variety, however. And remember that any technique you use for sentence variety will be self-defeating if you use it too often in a short piece of writing.

Chapter Checkout

Q&A

1. Identify the following as RO (run-on), Frag (fragment), or C correct sentence.

   a. Dr. Jamal Washington, a brilliant cardiologist, invented a surgical procedure that is still used in hospitals today.

   b. Although nothing prepared Miranda for the long week waiting for her test scores.

   c. Even though Jeff knew the birds were rare, he hoped they would survive, his mother treasured them.

2. Circle the correct verb form in the sentences.

   a. Neither Bill nor Eleanor is/are ready for the holidays.

   b. Harold as well as Jimmy drive/drives a new truck.

   c. Jenny, distracted by the falling snow, do/does not notice the traffic.

3. Select the best answer to correct the part of the sentence that is underlined:

a. Running the five mile marathon, <u>the rain began to drizzle and Wesley stopped</u>.

   1. the rain began to drizzle so Wesley stopped.
   2. Wesley stopped, being as the rain began to drizzle
   3. Wesley, the rain drizzling, stopped.
   4. Wesley felt the rain drizzling and stopped.

b. Determined to propose properly, Shawn decided to get a job that would pay more, which would allow him to invest in a new suit <u>by providing more money, and to plan</u> for a romantic evening.

   1. by providing more money, and to plan
   2. by providing more money, and planning
   3. to provide more money, and planning

c. His growing suspicion about Mrs. Baylor's affair <u>arose not from any specific event, but developed</u> over the summer.

   1. arose not from any specific event but developed
   2. did not arise from any specific event but developed
   3. was not arising from any specific event but developed

Answers: 1. a. C b. Frag c. RO 2. a. is b. drives c. does 3. a. 4 b. 1 c. 2.

Chapter 8

PERIODS, QUESTION MARKS, AND EXCLAMATION POINTS

Chapter Check-In

❏ Understanding when to use periods

❏ Avoiding problems with question marks

❏ Creating emphasis with exclamation points

As you write, you make use of periods, question marks, or exclamation points to end your sentences. Periods are used to complete most sentences while question marks end sentences that ask questions. Exclamation marks indicate statements of strong emphasis or emotion either in a command, an interjection, or a strongly worded sentence. Exclamation points, like dashes and parentheses, should be used sparingly for the greatest impact. You need to learn some basic rules in order to use these punctuation marks correctly.

Uses of the Period

Use **periods** to end complete sentences that are statements, commands and requests, or mild exclamations. There are a few simple rules in using the period as in the following examples.

> He spends winters in Florida and summers in Cape *Cod.*
>
> Please open your books to the third *chapter.*
>
> How odd it is to see Robert sitting in his father's *place.*

Don't use periods at the end of phrases or dependent clauses. If you do, you create sentence fragments.

> *When she visits cities in the East,* Mrs. Tuhy expects bad weather.
>
> NOT *When she visits cities in the East.* Mrs. Tuhy expects bad weather.

Courtesy questions

If a question is asked as a courtesy, you can use either a question mark or a period. Although the difference in tone is slight, the period makes the question more routine and general, the question mark more directed and personal.

> Would you please take your seat before the *bell*.
> Would you please take your seat before the *bell?*

Abbreviations

Most common abbreviations end in a period: *Mr., Mrs., a.m., etc., Tues., Sept.* But other abbreviations are written without a period, and modern practice is shifting more in that direction. In general, you can omit periods for abbreviations written in capital letters *(FBI, CIA, IOU, NBC)* if the abbreviation doesn't appear to spell out another word. For example, *USA* is acceptable, but *M.A.* should include periods, since it could be mistaken for a capitalization of the slang word *ma*. Most abbreviations that end in a lower-case letter should still be written with periods: *i.e., Dr., yr., mo.* Exceptions to this rule include *mph, rpm,* and metric measurement abbreviations such as *ml, cm, gm*. Do not use periods with zip code abbreviations for states: *AL, AZ, CA, NY, WY,* etc. If you are uncertain about using periods with a particular abbreviation, check a dictionary or style guide.

Periods with quotation marks

Always keep periods inside quotation marks, whether or not they are part of the quotation.

> Katie Jane said, "I didn't take the *money.*"
> Mr. Wolfe insisted on referring to his young girlfriend as his "little tootsie *pop.*"

In the first sentence, the period is part of the quoted sentence. In the second sentence the phrase *"little tootsie pop"* does not end in a period, but the period for the complete sentence still correctly appears within the quotation marks.

Punctuation with abbreviations

If a sentence ends with an abbreviation, use only one period.

He introduced his friend as Harold Ruiz, *M.D.*

Tula told her mother, "I won't be satisfied until I earn my *Ph.D.*"

Use of the Question Mark

Obviously, the role of the **question mark** is to end a question. The question mark immediately follows the question, even when one question interrupts or comes after a statement. For optional use of question marks with courtesy questions, see the beginning of this Chapter.

> *Who knows?*

> I spoke to her—*don't you remember?*—and she still refused to come.

> No doubt Mildred thought she was doing the right thing, *but can't we agree she was wrong?*

An exception to this rule occurs when the question is followed by a phrase or clause that modifies it. Then, put the question mark at the end of the statement.

> How could the mother be so certain of the driver's identity, *considering the shock she must have felt at seeing her own daughter lying in the road?*

Commas and periods with question marks

After a question mark, don't use a period or comma, even if your sentence would normally call for one. Too much punctuation can confuse the reader as in the following examples.

> Later Kevin understood what Gretchen meant when she asked, "*Why me?*"

> NOT Later Kevin understood what Gretchen meant when she asked, "*Why me?*".

> "Do you want to *go?*" Patty asked.

> NOT "Do you want to *go?*", Patty asked.

> Questions that end with abbreviations are an exception.

> Was it at precisely 4 *a.m.?*

Question marks with quotation marks

If the material being quoted is a question, put the question mark within the quotation marks.

"Do you think I'll get the job?" Susannah asked.

David looked around and said, *"Who can speak for the old man?"*

If the quotation is not a question, put the question mark outside the quotation marks. If the quoted material would normally end with a period, drop the period.

Who was it that said, "All that glitters is not gold"*?*

NOT *Who was it that said,* "All that glitters is not *gold.*"*?*

Problems with Question Marks

Two problem situations involving the use of question marks are the indirect question and the sarcastic, or emphatic, question. These are special cases that require you to be clear about your intent.

Indirect questions

When a question is being reported rather than directly asked, it ends with a period rather than a question mark. Compare the following sentences.

Ethan asked, "What made the sky so brilliant tonight?" (direct question)

Ethan asked what made the sky so brilliant tonight. (indirect question)

Sarcastic and emphatic question marks

Don't use question marks to indicate sarcasm (as in the first sentence). If you feel an overpowering need to call attention to the use of sarcasm, you can consider using quotation marks (as in the second sentence).

The actor said his interest in the orphans was purely altruistic *(?)* and that the presence of the photographers was coincidental. (not advisable)

The actor said his interest in the orphans was *"purely altruistic"* and that the presence of the photographers was coincidental. (better)

The phrase *"purely altruistic"* is probably a direct quote from the actor anyway. But be careful when using quotation marks to indicate tone; see the warnings in Chapter 10.

Never be tempted to use more than one question mark for the sake of emphasis.

Do you really want to risk your life skydiving?

NOT   Do you really want to risk your life skydiving??

The use of *really* makes the point.

Use of the Exclamation Point

Exclamation points follow interjections (see Chapter 5) and other expressions of strong feeling. They may also be used to lend force to a command.

What a mess!

The lights! The music! The dazzling costumes! My eyes and ears couldn't get enough of the spectacle.

Sit down and shut your mouth! Now!

An exclamation point is particularly useful if you're writing dialogue because it shows the feeling behind a statement.

Exclamation points with quotation marks

If the material being quoted is an exclamation, put the exclamation mark within the quotation marks.

"I hate you!" she screamed.

"What rubbish!" he said, leaving the room.

If an exclamation includes a quotation that is not an exclamation, put the mark outside the quotation marks.

For the last time, *stop calling me your "darling little boy"!*

Exclamation points with commas and periods

After an exclamation point, omit a comma or a period.

"You adorable thing*!*" he gushed.

NOT   "You adorable thing*!,*" he gushed.

What a terrible way to end our trip*!*

NOT   What a terrible way to end our trip*!.*

Problems with Exclamation Points

In formal writing, be careful. Overuse of exclamation points not only dulls their effect, but also characterizes an immature style.

> The film's last scene poignantly showed that his battle had been for nothing, that he had lost her and his dream forever.

> NOT The film's last scene was so *poignant!* You knew he'd lost her forever. His dream was *dead!*

Also, avoid using an exclamation point in parentheses to indicate sarcasm or irony; instead, rely on good writing to create the desired effect.

> Mother believed Mary's problem could be solved with a new dress, and she refused to discuss the issue further.

> NOT Mother believed Mary's problem could be solved with a new dress *(!)*, and she refused to discuss the issue further.

Chapter Checkout

Q&A

1. Insert the question mark or exclamation point in the correct location in the following sentences. If further punctuation is not needed write NP in the blank.

   a. "Hey ____" ____ Rebecca cried.

   b. Chip asked, "When does the bus leave ____" ____

   c. The candidate claimed the embezzlement was accidental _____, but we knew better.

   d. Sick of winter, Susan asked when the snow would stop _____

2. Insert a period, question mark, or quotation mark in the appropriate blank. If punctuation is not needed write NP.

   a. "Surprise _____" Mrs. Farrell's class cried in unison_____

   b. Amanda's birthday is Monday_____—have you forgotten_____

   c. Mr. Hughes said, "The car will be ready today____" ____

3. True or False: The following sentences are all correct uses of periods.

   a. He lied about his health. He wanted to protect her feelings.

   b. Even though she lost. Anna was a good sport.

   c. Mr. Spence told Tom, "Leave your plans with our client.'.

   d. He told us, "Natasha is now working on her M.A.".

   e. Evelyn called Caleb Jones, M.D.

Answers: 1. a. !, NP b. ?, NP c. NP d. period 2. a. !, period b. NP, ? c. period, NP 3. a. True b. False c. False d. False e. True.

Chapter 9

COMMAS, SEMICOLONS, AND COLONS

Chapter Check-In

❑ Learning the rules for commas

❑ Using semicolons in sentences

❑ Introducing the colon

Commas are useful for indicating pauses or brief breaks within your ideas. They add pacing to your sentences and make them clearer. Many beginning writers either neglect to use or overuse commas, which complicates their sentences, or can sometimes obscure their meaning. The rules for commas are simple and not difficult to learn.

The semicolon and colon are often confused and sometimes overused. The main rule for these punctuation marks is to use them sparingly. Semicolons join independent clauses and items in a series, and colons are used to introduce a list, a quote or formal statement; and to introduce a restatement or explanation. Once you master the rules for effective punctuation, your writing will improve accordingly.

Uses of the Comma

Commas are always used to join independent clauses, after introductory clauses and phrases, to set off interruptions within the sentence, with non-restrictive phrases and clauses, and between items or modifiers in a series. There are some special situations in which commas should also be used. For example, use commas with quotations, dates, addresses, locations, and numbers with four or more digits. Commas should never be used around restrictive clauses or to separate a subject and verb, or a verb and its direct object.

The best way to approach commas is, first, to recognize that they signal a pause, and, second, to know which rules can be bent without jarring or misleading your reader and which ones cannot. The comma is the most frequently used internal punctuation in sentences, and people have more questions about it than about any other punctuation mark. One reason is that different editors have different opinions about when a comma is needed. You're likely to read one book in which commas abound and another in which they are scarce. Generally, the trend has been towards lighter punctuation, and this trend means fewer commas. Rules that you may have learned in grammar school have been bent and are still bending.

Sometimes a comma is absolutely necessary to ensure the meaning of a sentence, as in the following examples.

> Because I wanted to *help, Dr. Hodges,* I pulled the car over to the side of the road.

> Because I wanted to *help Dr. Hodges,* I pulled the car over to the side of the road.

In the first sentence, the pair of commas indicates that Dr. Hodges is being addressed. In the second sentence, Dr. Hodges is the object of the help. Most situations, however, aren't this clear cut.

Joining independent clauses

Generally, when you join independent clauses with a coordinating conjunction, precede the conjunction with a comma.

> Lenin never answered these charges, *but* soon afterward he was compelled to give up part of the money.

> The novel lacks fully developed characters, *and* the plot is filled with unlikely coincidences.

If the two independent clauses are short and closely related, you may use a comma or omit it, depending on whether or not you want to indicate a pause.

> It was an admirable *scheme and* it would work.

OR It was an admirable *scheme, and* it would work.

> The night was *cold and* the sky was clear.

NOT The night was *cold, and* the sky was clear.

Remember that when you do use a comma between independent clauses, it *must* be accompanied by one of the coordinating conjunctions. If it isn't, you create a run-on sentence (see Chapter 7).

It had been a tumultuous year that had taken everybody by
surprise, and it left the revolutionaries worse off than they had
been before.

NOT It had been a tumultuous year that had taken everybody by
surprise, it left the revolutionaries worse off than they had been
before.

After introductory clauses

It is customary to use a comma after an introductory adverbial clause. (For
adverbial clauses, see Chapter 6.) With a lengthy clause, the comma is
essential.

After she walked into the room, we stopped gossiping.

If you receive inappropriate material, acknowledge it by explaining to
the correspondent why the material won't see print.

With today's trend towards light punctuation, you may omit the comma if
the subordinate clause is short, and if there is no possibility for confusion.

When she arrived we stopped gossiping.

After I was sixteen I was allowed to stay out until midnight.

Be sure that omitting a comma will not lead your reader to a momentary
misunderstanding. Look at the example below.

When we are cooking children cannot come into the kitchen. (no)

When we are cooking, children cannot come into the kitchen. (yes)

Without a comma, your reader may suspect you of cannibalism.

After introductory phrases

Remember that, unlike a clause, a phrase is a group of words without a
subject and a predicate (see Chapter 6).

If an introductory phrase is more than a few words, it's a good idea to follow it with a comma. And always use a comma if there is any possibility
of misunderstanding a sentence without one.

By taking the initiative to seek out story leads, a reporter will make a
good impression on the editor.

At the beginning of the visiting professor's lecture, most of the students
were wide awake.

Unlike so many performances of the symphony, this one was spirited
and lively.

Before eating, Jack always runs on the beach.

Note that the introductory phrase in the last example, although short, would lead to a momentary misunderstanding if the comma were omitted.

A participial phrase at the beginning of a sentence is *always* followed by a comma.

> *Smiling and shaking hands,* the senator worked her way through the crowd.

Do not confuse a participial phrase with a gerund phrase, however (see Chapter 6). A gerund phrase that begins a sentence would not be followed by a comma. Compare the following two sentences.

> *Thinking of the consequences,* she agreed not to release the memo to the press. (introductory participial phrase, modifying *she:* use a comma)
>
> *Thinking of the consequences* gave her a tremendous headache. (gerund phrase, functioning as the subject of the sentence: do *not* use a comma)

Use of a comma after most short introductory phrases is optional.

> *Later that day* Jack and Linda drove to the ocean.
>
> *After the main course* I was too full for dessert.
>
> *For some unknown reason* the car wouldn't start.

The best way to decide whether to use a comma is to read your sentence aloud and see whether you pause distinctly after the introductory phrase. Use a comma if you do.

To set off interrupting elements

Some phrases, clauses, and terms interrupt the flow of a sentence and should be enclosed in commas. Examples of these interrupters are conjunctive adverbs, transitional phrases (see Chapter 7), and names in direct address.

Conjunctive adverbs and transitional phrases—such as consequently, as a matter of fact, of course, therefore, on the other hand, for example, however, to tell the truth, moreover—are usually followed by commas when they begin sentences.

> *For example,* you shouldn't use the solution on soft surfaces.
>
> *Therefore,* he refused to go with us.

When they interrupt a sentence, they are usually enclosed in commas.

As the project moves along, *of course,* you will be given greater independence.

One who is strong at research, *for example,* might be assigned to the library.

Know what your intention is. If you want the reader to pause, use the commas. If you don't, omit them. Look at the following two examples.

The committee, *therefore,* agreed to hear the students.

The committee *therefore* agreed to hear the students.

Both sentences are correct. In the second sentence the expression would be read as part of the flow of the sentence, not as an interrupter.

A name or expression used in direct address is always followed by a comma, or enclosed in commas when it interrupts the sentence.

Friends, I am here to ask for your support.

I tell you, *Mr. Smith,* I will not be forced into this by you or anyone.

Yes, *readers,* I am telling you the truth.

Other interrupters may also require commas. Check your sentence for elements outside the main flow of the sentence and enclose them in commas.

It is too early, *I believe,* to call in the police.

The historical tour, *we were led to believe,* was organized by experts.

Dashes and parentheses can also be used to set off some kinds of interrupting elements (see Chapter 10), but commas are better when you want to draw less attention to an interruption.

With restrictive and nonrestrictive elements

Look at the following two sentences. In the first sentence, *who arrived yesterday* is a *restrictive* clause, that is, one that restricts, limits, or defines the subject of the sentence. In the second sentence, the same clause is *nonrestrictive,* that is, it doesn't restrict or narrow the meaning but instead adds information. In the simplest terms, a restrictive element is essential to the reader's understanding; a nonrestrictive element is not.

The women *who arrived yesterday* toured the island this afternoon.

The women, *who arrived yesterday,* toured the island this afternoon.

In the first sentence, *who arrived yesterday* defines exactly which women are the subject of the sentence, separating them from all other women. In the second sentence, however, the information *who arrived yesterday* is not necessary to the sentence. It does not separate the women from all other women. The clause adds information, but the information isn't essential to our knowing which women are being discussed. It is you, as writer, who must decide which kind of information you intend to give.

Commas make all the difference in meaning here. Restrictive (or essential) elements shouldn't be enclosed in commas, while nonrestrictive (or nonessential) elements should be. Review the following sentences.

> The workers *who went on strike* were replaced. (restrictive)

> The workers, *who went on strike,* were replaced. (nonrestrictive)

In the first sentence, only some workers were replaced. The absence of commas restricts the subject to only those workers who went on strike. In the second sentence, all the workers were replaced. The information that they went on strike is not essential; it doesn't define exactly which workers were replaced.

In the following sentence, the phrase *who are over fifty* is essential in limiting the subject *men* and therefore should not be enclosed in commas. The second sentence means that all men are over fifty, which is absurd.

> Men *who are over fifty* have difficulty finding a new job.

> NOT Men, *who are over fifty,* have difficulty finding a new job.

Whether to use commas around modifying elements is based entirely on whether the element is restrictive (essential or limiting) or nonrestrictive (added information).

> My brother, *who is thirteen,* watches television more than he reads. (added information)

> The man *who took the pictures* is being sued for invasion of privacy. (essential)

> Cats, *more independent than dogs,* are good pets for people who work all day. (added information)

> Cats *who are fussy eaters* are a trial to their owners. (essential)

> My brother, *swimming in the ocean,* saw a shark. (added information)

> People *swimming in the ocean* should watch for sharks. (essential)

With appositives

Appositives are words that restate or identify a noun or pronoun (see Chapter 3). When appositives, are nonrestrictive, they are enclosed in commas.

Kublai Khan, *grandson of Genghis,* was the first Mongol emperor of all China.

Jack Kerouac, *one of the most famous of the Beat Generation writers,* came to symbolize the era he wrote about.

Patricia Mack, *my old friend from college,* became a successful writer.

Sometimes, however, an appositive is essential because it limits the subject. It must *not,* therefore, be enclosed in commas. Look at the following examples.

Shakespeare's play *Hamlet* was probably written about 1600.

NOT   Shakespeare's play, *Hamlet,* was probably written about 1600.

In this example, if you enclose *Hamlet* in commas, you suggest that Shakespeare wrote only one play. Obviously, the appositive *Hamlet* is restrictive; it limits the subject *play.*

Between items in a series

Use commas to separate items in a series. Although some editors feel that it is acceptable to omit the final comma in a series—journalists and business writers frequently do—it is safer not to.

He bought a *dishwasher, microwave, refrigerator, and washer* from the outlet.

Her play is filled with *coincidences, false anticipations, and non-responsive dialogue.*

Omitting a final comma may create ambiguity, and since you should be consistent throughout a piece of writing, why not consistently use the final comma and avoid possible problems?

Hair, clothing and jewelry all send messages to a prospective employer. (acceptable)

Hair, clothing, and jewelry all send messages to a prospective employer. (better)

She told us about the *subway, the elevators at Bloomingdale's and the Metropolitan Museum of Art.* (ambiguous: the elevators at both Bloomingdale's and the Metropolitan Museum or just at Bloomingdale's?)

She told us about the *subway, the elevators at Bloomingdale's, and the Metropolitan Museum of Art.* (better)

Don't use commas if all items in a series are joined by *and* or *or*

> He asked to see *Martha and Helen and Eileen.*
>
> NOT He asked to see *Martha, and Helen, and Eileen.*

Between modifiers in a series

Modifiers in a series are usually separated with commas. But don't put a comma between the final modifier and the word it modifies.

> It was a *dark, gloomy, forbidding* house.
>
> NOT It was a *dark, gloomy, forbidding,* house.

In this example, all three modifiers—*dark, gloomy,* and *forbidding*—modify *house.*

Sometimes, however, what seems to be a modifier is actually part of the element being modified. Look at the following examples.

> He is a *tall, good-looking, intelligent young man.*

Young man, not just *man,* is the element being modified. Therefore, don't use a comma after *intelligent.*

> They bought a *beautiful, spacious summer home.*

Summer home, not just *home,* is being modified. Don't use a comma after *spacious.*

To test whether you should use a comma before the last adjective in a series, see if it makes sense to reverse the order of the adjectives. If you can reverse them without changing the meaning or eliminating sense, then use commas between them. If you can't, don't.

> It was a *dark, gloomy, forbidding* house.
>
> It was a *forbidding, dark, gloomy* house. (no change in meaning)

The order of the adjectives can change; therefore, use commas between them.

> They bought a *beautiful, spacious summer* home.
>
> They bought a *summer, beautiful, spacious* home. (does not make sense)

By changing the order of the adjectives, the sentence becomes nonsensical. Therefore, you would not use a comma between *spacious* and *summer.*

Commas with quotation marks

Commas go inside quotation marks, whether or not they are part of the quotation.

> He called her *"that fiend from Hell,"* and he sent a series of threatening letters.

> "I can't believe you ate the entire *watermelon*," she said.

Miscellaneous uses of the comma

There are some special situations where you should use commas. For example, commas are used in the following instances:

■ To present quotations, with *he said, she muttered, etc.*

> *He said,* "Let's go."

> "Wait a while," *she said,* "and I will."

■ Between items in dates and addresses (except between state and zip code)

> *1328 Say Road, Santa Paula, CA 93060*

> *December 10, 1902*

■ Between cities and counties, cities and states, states and countries

> *Boise, Idaho*

■ To set off items in dates and addresses within sentences

> *December 10, 1902,* is his birthday.

> *He lived at 23 Park Street, Boise, Idaho,* until he left for Chiapas, Mexico.

■ In numbers of more than four digits

> *50,000*

> *293,456,678*

■ After salutations and closings in letters

> *Dear Judith,*

> *Yours truly,*

■ To enclose a title or degree

> Jeff Nelson, *LL.D.,* spoke at the dinner.

Problems with Commas

The main mistake people make with commas is putting them where they absolutely don't belong.

Don't use commas around restrictive elements.

> The novel *Naked Lunch* was banned from the school library.
> NOT The novel, *Naked Lunch,* was banned from the school library.

Don't separate subject from verb with a comma.

> The *girl in the window is* not my sister.
> NOT The *girl in the window, is* not my sister.

Don't separate a verb and a direct object or complement with a comma.

> I *saw immediately the mistake* I had made.
> NOT I *saw immediately, the mistake* I had made.

When your sentence includes paired elements—for example, with correlative conjunctions—don't use a comma to separate them.

> I wanted *either a trip to Europe or a new Mercedes.*
> NOT I *wanted either a trip to Europe, or a new Mercedes.*

In other situations when you are unsure about using a comma, don't add one out of insecurity. Check the rules first, and if the answer isn't there, count on your own ear to tell you when a pause is important.

Uses of the Semicolon

Beginning writers often mistakenly use semicolons to connect fragments or sentences that really should have been two separate sentences. Use the **semicolon** to connect two independent clauses or a series of items.

Joining independent clauses

A semicolon is much like a period, but whereas a period keeps two independent clauses apart and turns them into separate sentences, a semicolon joins them to show a close connection. Compare the following examples.

> I helped the committee all I *could.* *I* even searched the back issues of the paper to find evidence.

> I helped the committee all I *could; I* even searched the back issues of the paper to find evidence.

I helped the committee all I *could, and* I even searched the back issues of the paper to find evidence.

All three examples are correct. The semicolon emphasizes a close relationship between the two independent clauses.

Often you'll find a conjunctive adverb or transitional phrase (see Chapter 7) in the clause following a semicolon, since those words point out the relationship between the clauses.

The results of the inquiry were *unclear; however,* the head of the project resigned.

Some people continued to support *us;* others, *on the other hand,* refused to speak to us.

Indicators like these aren't required. But don't use a semicolon unless you want to emphasize the close connection between clauses.

It was time to *vote;* we were sick of the endless wrangling. (yes)

It was time to *vote;* the secretary carried lunch in and put it on the table. (no, unless the vote concerns lunch)

You may follow a semicolon that divides independent clauses with one of the seven coordinating conjunctions (see Chapter 5), although it is not necessary to do so as it is when you separate independent clauses with a comma.

That night the timber wolf appeared to *revive; but* when we woke in the morning, full of hope that we had saved it, we were saddened to find its body at the edge of the clearing.

It would be perfectly correct to use a comma before *but* in this example; the semicolon, however, creates a stronger pause. Also, because there are already two commas in the second clause, a semicolon in desirable, since it indicates the main break in the sentence.

Between items in a series

In a series, use a semicolon between items if the items are particularly long, or if they themselves contain commas.

The planning committee included David H. Takahashi, president of the Kiwanis *Club;* Leroy Carter, head of the local merchants *group;* Romana Gilbert, editor of the local *paper;* and Irma Quintero, Spanish department chairperson at the junior college.

Jesse Stone's report states that the college, plagued by financial worries, cannot fulfill these *needs;* that the community response, while positive, has not resulted in substantial *donations;* and that charitable organizations, service clubs, and private donors have been overwhelmed with similar requests.

Notice that when semicolons are used in series, the series' items do not have to be independent clauses.

Semicolons with quotation marks

Follow this rule when dealing with quotation marks: always place semicolons outside the quotation mark.

> He asked me to be quiet and mind my *"atrocious manners"*; I told him I'd say what I pleased.

> Mrs. Coot wanted to use words like "prohibit" and *"forbid";* to devise strong, painful punishments for *infractions;* to publish this book of rules as soon as *possible;* and, in a bountiful gesture, to distribute it to the orphans on Christmas Eve along with their gruel.

Problems with semicolons

Except when used to separate items in a series, a semicolon must be followed by an independent clause or you create a sentence fragment.

> I expected to win the debate*; even if my opponent had more experience.* (sentence fragment)

> I had studied the subject thoroughly*; and researched even the minor points.* (sentence fragment)

These sentences could be corrected either by changing punctuation or by making the second clause independent.

> I expected to win the *debate, even* if my opponent had more experience.

> I had studied the subject *thoroughly; I* had researched even the minor points.

Uses of the Colon

A **colon** is used to introduce a list. It can be a formal introduction using *as follows,* or less formal.

> The ceremony to honor Dr. Mills included *everything:* a moving introduction, a recitation of her achievements, a series of testimonials, and a stirring forecast of her future in the new position.

The questions were *as follows:* Where did you last work? For how long? What was your job title? What were your primary achievements?

As follows and *following* are clear indications that a colon is appropriate, but as the first example shows, these formal introductory elements aren't required. Also, use a lower-case letter after the colon unless your list is made up of complete statements, as in the second example.

Introducing a quotation or formal statement

The colon is used to introduce a quotation or formal statement. An independent clause must precede the colon. The statement following the colon begins with a capital letter.

> *Remember this:* Don't waste time, don't waste money, but—most important of all—don't waste your energies and talents.

> *The speaker made the following observation:* "In the future, communication between people all over the world will lead not to an enriched culture but to a homogenous one."

Introducing a restatement or explanation

A colon may be used between two independent clauses when the second clause explains or restates the first clause.

> The program was an unqualified success: *hundreds of people attended.*

> These shoes are the best: *they are durable, inexpensive, and stylish.*

Notice that when the colon is used in this way, it may be followed by a lower-case letter, just as a semicolon would be.

To test whether you should use a semicolon or a colon between clauses, ask yourself whether you could insert the phrase *that is* after the mark. If you can, use a colon; if you can't, use a semicolon.

> These shoes are the best: *that is,* they are durable, inexpensive, and stylish. (yes)

A colon is appropriate in the previous example. The phrase can be inserted here. The second clause explains the first clause. The phrase *that is* doesn't work in the next sentence. A semicolon is appropriate.

> He struggled for years; *that is,* success finally arrived. (no)

> He struggled for years; *success* finally arrived. (yes)

Colons with quotation marks

Follow this rule when using quotes in a sentence: always place colons outside quotation marks.

> The article was called "The Last *Word*": it was his definitive statement.
>
> This statement is from an article called "Good *Advice*": "Before you decide to marry a man, check out his relationship with his mother."

Miscellaneous uses of the colon

You also need to learn some special cases for using a colon. A colon is used in the following situations:

- To separate hours and minutes when writing the time

    4:15 p.m.

    8:00 a.m.

- To separate volume and number, or volume and page number of a magazine

    Entertainment Weekly VI:4

    Newsweek 87:53-56

- To separate chapter and verse numbers for biblical passages

    Matthew 4:16

- To introduce a subtitle

    Jane Austen: A Feminist's View

- To end the salutation of a business letter

    Dear Dr. Aguinaldo:

Problems with Colons

Don't use a colon to separate sentence elements that belong together, such as an action verb from its objects or a linking verb from its complements.

> The university sent *us catalogues,* maps, housing applications, and transportation information.
>
> NOT The university sent *us: catalogues,* maps, housing applications, and transportation information.

The four things I want *are success* in business, a happy marriage, creative fulfillment, and peace of mind.

NOT The four things I want *are: success* in business, a happy marriage, creative fulfillment, and peace of mind.

Chapter Checkout

Q&A

1. Place commas in the appropriate locations in the sentences below.

a. Derek and Barbara who both graduated from Princeton are expecting their first baby a girl in April.

b. My new sister-in-law Hong Anh will be flying in from Hanoi Vietnam today.

c. Even though the weather was warm the seeds did not sprout.

d. I read about the Mayans a fascinating culture in Mexico.

e. As a matter of fact the loggerhead turtles are endangered.

f. Sabitha said "Call before noon."

2. Identify whether the following sentences require an (S) semicolon or a (C) colon.

a. To be a good hostess, you must consider food everyone loves to eat at parties.

b. The award show featured rap musicians, pop musicians, two alternative bands, and even some jazz artists.

c. I cleaned my room thoroughly I even cleaned out the closet.

d. He is thoughtful he never forgets my birthday.

3. True or False: The following sentences are all correct uses of commas.

a. "Don't be late," she exclaimed.

b. The ship, City on the Sea, docked last night.

c. The hospital, on the hill, is where I was born.

d. Betty cautiously held, the antique vase.

e. William Sheehy, our postman, was born in Ireland.

Answers: 1. a. Derek and Barbara, who both graduated from Princeton, are expecting their first baby, a girl, in April. b. My new sister-in-law, Hong Anh, will be flying in from Hanoi, Vietnam today. c. Even though the weather was warm, the seeds did not sprout. d. I read about the Mayans, a fascinating culture in Mexico. e. As a matter of fact, the loggerhead turtles are endangered. f. Sabitha said, "Call before noon." 2. a. Semicolon b. Colon c. Colon d. Semicolon 3. a. True b. False c. True d. False e. True.

Chapter 10

DASHES, PARENTHESES, AND QUOTATION MARKS

Chapter Check-In

❑ Knowing when to use a dash

❑ Using parentheses correctly

❑ Learning the rules for quotation marks

Dashes and parentheses are interruptions within the sentence that can provide extra information. In many cases they may be necessary and valuable additions. Brackets are used only when inserting material into parentheses or around a word or phrase of your own that is added to a quote.

Beginning writers are sometimes tempted to overuse these devices. Generally, your writing should be direct and well organized, which means you will use dashes or parentheses sparingly.

Uses of the Dash

Think of the **dash** as indicating an interruption you want to draw attention to. Other punctuation marks—commas and parentheses—serve similar purposes. Commas are more neutral, and parentheses are usually used with information that is clearly incidental.

Interrupting a sentence

If you want to interrupt your sentence with a phrase or clause, consider using a dash, or if your sentence continues after the interruption, a pair of dashes.

> She was extraordinarily tall—*the tallest woman I'd ever seen.*
>
> She walked in—*the tallest woman I'd ever seen*—and took a seat at the counter.

Introducing a restatement or explanation

Like a colon, a dash can be used to introduce an explanation or restatement in place of expressions such as *that is, in other words,* or *namely.* Begin the clause after the dash with a lower-case letter.

> The reporter relentlessly pursued the woman—*he was determined to get her to respond.*

Although the colon and dash are frequently interchangeable in this function, the dash is less formal.

Dashes with commas

When you use dashes to set off interrupting elements in a sentence, omit commas.

> She saw her sisters—*all five of them*—*standing* in front of the building.
>
> NOT She saw her sisters,—*all five of them*—, *standing* in front of the building.

Dashes with quotation marks

If a dash is not part of the quoted material, put it outside the quotation marks. Omit commas.

> "He wants the money"—*I paused for effect*—"and he wants it now."

A dash can be used to indicate unfinished dialogue. Put the dash within the quotation marks and omit commas or periods.

> "*Help! Help! I can't seem to*—" She fell to the ground, gasping for breath.

Problems with Dashes

If you like dashes, you'll be tempted to use them too often. Remember that they are more noticeable than commas. Then remember a basic rule: Don't let a punctuation mark become a distraction.

When you type, don't confuse a dash with a hyphen. A dash is typed with two hyphens, no space between them, or typed as a dash with a word processor.

> Ms. Persinger--*the most important official in the city*--okayed the plan.
>
> OR Ms. Persinger—*the most important official in the city*—*okayed* the plan. (better)

NOT Ms. Persinger-*the most important official in the city*-okayed the plan.

Uses of Parentheses

Parentheses are a pair of signs ( ) helpful in marking off text. You use parentheses in specific situations that can be covered by a few simple rules.

Setting off incidental information

Parentheses are used to enclose incidental information, such as a passing comment, a minor example or addition, or a brief explanation. As with the dash, the decision to use parentheses is your judgment call. Sometimes commas or dashes might be a better choice.

> Some of the local store owners *(Mr. Kwan and Ms. Lawson, for example)* insisted that the street be widened,

OR Some of the local store owners—*Mr. Kwan and Ms. Lawson, for example*—insisted that the street be widened.

> Roger Worthington (*a poorly drawn character in the novel*) reveals the secret in the last chapter.

OR Roger Worthington, *a poorly drawn character in the novel,* reveals the secret in the last chapter.

Other punctuation marks with parentheses

Don't put any punctuation mark before parentheses, and put a comma after the closing parenthesis only if your sentence would call for the comma anyway.

> Use a pointed stick *(a pencil with the lead point broken off works well)* or a similar tool.

No comma appears before or after the parentheses. If you were to remove the parenthetical remark, the remaining sentence would not need a comma: *Use a pointed stick or a similar tool.*

> Banging the wall and screaming *(unrestrained by his father, I might add),* Sam was acting like a brat.

In the preceding sentence, no comma appears before the parentheses. A comma follows the parentheses because if you were to remove the parenthetical comment, the remaining sentence would require a comma: *Banging the wall and screaming, Sam was acting like a brat.*

Punctuation within parentheses

If your parentheses enclose a sentence-within-a-sentence, don't use a period within the parentheses. Do, however, use a question mark or an exclamation point if it is called for.

Mother love *(hers was fierce)* ruined the young boy's life.

They finally said *(why couldn't they have admitted it earlier?)* that she had been there.

The wedding reception *(what a fiasco!)* ended abruptly.

If the parentheses enclose a complete sentence that stands alone, keep the period within the parentheses.

(Her father was the only one who didn't attend.)

Miscellaneous uses of parentheses

You'll need to learn how to use parentheses in special situations. For example, use parentheses to enclose a date or a citation.

Sir William Walton *(1902–1983)* composed the oratorio *Belshazzar's Feast*.

According to the reports of her contemporaries, she was a mediocre critic and a worse artist *(Travis, 26–62)*.

In scientific, business, or legal writing, parentheses are used to restate a number. Be sure this use is justified. In most prose, it is not, and it creates an inappropriately official tone.

The bill is due and payable in *thirty (30)* days. (acceptable)

My grandfather knew my grandmother for *sixty (60)* years. (not appropriate)

When to use brackets

Brackets are a special case and are used in specific situations. Use brackets to insert something into a sentence that is already in parentheses.

(Don't forget, however, that the joints will be filled with grout *[see page 46].)*

Also use brackets when you want to insert an explanatory word or note within a quotation.

"Mel *[Gibson]* is one of my best customers," the street vendor bragged.

Problems with Parentheses

Like dashes, parentheses are punctuation marks with high visibility, so don't overuse them. If you find yourself putting much information in parentheses, check the way you have organized your material. Generally, your writing should be straightforward, not filled with asides or passing comments.

Uses of Quotation Marks

Quotation marks are used to indicate the beginning and end of a quote. They tell the reader when you've used written material from other sources or direct speech.

Direct quotations

A direct quotation is when you've used an item verbatim from another text. Use quotation marks at the beginning and end of a direct quotation.

> "*You are the last person on earth I'd ask,*" she told him.

When you are incorporating a short quotation into a paper or thesis, use quotation marks and quote the material exactly.

> As film critic Pauline Kael writes, "*At his greatest, Jean Renoir expresses the beauty in our common humanity—the desires and hopes, the absurdities and follies, that we all, to one degree or another, share.*"

In a double-spaced paper, indent and single space quotations longer than five typed lines.

Quotations within quotations

Use single quotation marks within double ones to indicate a quotation within a quotation.

> "*My father began by saying, 'I refuse to listen to any excuses,'*" he told the psychiatrist.

If you are indenting and single spacing a quoted passage, however, use the same marks that appear in the passage. In the following example, the writer is quoting a passage from the critic Martin Esslin who in turn is quoting the playwright Ionesco.

> Martin Esslin describes Ionesco's attitude towards spontaneity in this passage:

Ionesco regards spontaneity as an important creative element. *"I have no ideas before I write a play. I have them when I have written the play or while I am not writing at all. I believe that artistic creation is spontaneous. It certainly is so for me."* But this does not mean that he considers his writing to be meaningless or without significance. On the contrary, the workings of the spontaneous imagination are a cognitive process, an exploration.

Miscellaneous uses of quotation marks

Except to indicate direct quotations, use quotation marks sparingly. However, there are a few other possible uses of quotation marks.

Distancing yourself from an offensive term or expression.

> The disappointed body builder blamed the *"fat slobs"* who judged the contest.

Referring to a word as a word.

> He used the term *"irregardless,"* not realizing that no such word exists.

Indicating a nickname written as part of a formal name.

> Ray *"Shorty"* Johannsen was the men's unanimous choice for chairman.

Setting off titles of poems, essays, and articles that are part of a longer work. (For this use, as for bibliographical and footnote information, check to see whether you are required to use a particular style guide for what you are writing.)

A summary of the rules

One of the biggest problems with quotation marks is knowing whether another mark, such as a period or comma, goes inside or outside the quotation marks. Following is a summary of the rules:

- Put periods and commas inside quotation marks, whether or not they are part of the quotation.

- Put question marks, exclamation points, and dashes inside quotation marks if they are part of the quotation, outside the quotation marks if they are not.

- Put colons and semicolons outside quotation marks.

For examples, look under the individual punctuation marks covered in this section.

Using an ellipsis

An **ellipsis** indicates an omission from a quotation. This mark consists of spaced periods.

A three-dot ellipsis indicates that you are omitting something from a sentence that continues after the ellipsis.

> He writes, "*The wise collector should probably just bite the bullet . . . and acquire both paintings.*"

The phrase "or mortgage the house" has been omitted from this quotation.

Use four dots if you are omitting the last part of a quoted sentence that ends in a period but what remains is still a complete thought. The first dot comes immediately after the sentence and has no space before it. It functions as a period. The following three dots are spaced and indicate that material has been omitted. If the original sentence ended in a question mark or exclamation point, substitute that mark for the first dot.

> The author advises, "*In analyzing nonverbal signals, look at the total pattern of behavior rather than just one symbol. . . .*"

The phrase "before making a decision," which ended the sentence, has been omitted from this quotation.

You can also use the four-dot ellipsis whenever your quotation skips material and then goes on to a new sentence. But make sure that your four-dot ellipsis has an independent clause on each side of it.

Problems with Quotation Marks

Aside from understanding how to use other punctuation marks with quotation marks, you shouldn't have much difficulty—if you keep one thing in mind. Reserve quotation marks for direct quotations and for the other uses indicated above. Don't use quotation marks around the title of your paper. Don't use them to signal—and somehow justify—the use of clichés or slang expressions. Don't use them to indicate that you are being clever or cute. In fact, don't use them to call attention to your tone at all unless you find it absolutely necessary to do so. You must be the judge, and you must be a harsh one. A piece of writing peppered with questionable quotation marks indicates an amateurish style.

Chapter Checkout

Q&A

1. Choose the correct location for punctuation in the following sentences. If punctuation is not needed write NP in the blank.

   a. Minh stated, "The results are in____"____
   b. The study revealed, "Wages are down . . .____"____
   c. He cried, "Hold the door____"____
   d. Bridget asked, "When will we stop ____"____
   e. "Now is the time____"____we must act today____

2. True or False: The following sentences could be corrected by the addition of a dash or a parentheses.

   a. Lost in the museum the second one we visited Mark never panicked.
   b. Even though Carlton was well qualified, he lost the election.
   c. My cousin Sara is a dancer a great dancer.
   d. Mrs. Millick was rude and not for the first time to my wife.

3. True or False: The following sentences are all correct usages of quotation marks.

   a. The term "generation X" was coined recently.
   b. As the movie ended, he whispered, "Let's go."
   c. Dr. Schwartz cited a study which claimed, "Life exists on Mars."
   d. Claire read aloud, "When playing basketball the key is endurance. . . . "

Answers: 1. a. Minh stated, "The results are in." NP b. The study revealed, "Wages are down. . . ." NP c. He cried, "Hold the door!" NP d. Bridget asked, "When will we stop?" NP e. "Now is the time."; we must act today. 2 a. True b. False c. True d. True 3. a. True b. True c. True d. False.

Chapter 11

IDIOMS, CLICHÉS, JARGON, AND FADDISH LANGUAGE

Chapter Check-In

❑ Recognizing idioms

❑ Learning how to use clichés

❑ Avoiding jargon, faddish language, and slang

❑ Identifying euphemisms

As a writer, you must choose your language carefully. Unclear or careless language affects your ability to communicate. It is important for you to recognize words or expressions that weaken your message in order to avoid them in your writing.

Idioms are expressions that do not have a literal meaning, but establish their connotation by the way they are used in speech. Clichés are expressions that are so commonly used they fail to impart any real impact on your sentence. Jargon is the specialized, often technical, language of a particular field or profession. Slang is the informal language of conversation, which includes contractions, faddish language, and other casual language. Euphemisms are mild or softer words or phrases used to blunt the effect of more direct or unpleasant words or phrases. If you know when to use or avoid these expressions, your writing will be more effective.

The Idiom

An **idiom** is an accepted phrase or expression that doesn't follow the usual patterns of the language or that has a meaning other than the literal. Phrases that, when dissected, don't seem to make much sense, are often idiomatic. For example, when you read "They can't *come up with* the answer," or "The director *stood up for* herself," or "They promise to *drop you a line,*" you know what the writer means. But if you look up each word in one of these expressions, the meaning of the expression as a whole isn't obvious.

Idioms aren't something you memorize; it would take you a lifetime. If English is your native language, you've already learned thousands of them naturally so that you don't need to question what they mean—or how they mean what they mean. But when you try to learn the idioms of another language, or when you ask someone who is trying to learn English, you find that idioms can be a real challenge.

Figurative idioms

Figurative idioms are expressions so common you don't question their source: *let the cat out of the bag; he has a monkey on his back; it's the straw that broke the camel's back; you're splitting hairs; the ball's in your court;* etc. Many figurative idioms have become clichés. You can use them occasionally, when they do a job for you—but don't overuse them. Also, be sure you know what they mean and that you use them correctly. Don't make the mistake of the real-estate agent who told her client, *"The monkey's in your court now."*

Prepositional idioms

The most common idiom is an expression that depends on the choice of a particular preposition. The choice may seem arbitrary. For example, why do we say "She *put up with* him" rather than "She *put on* with him"? *"At home"* rather than *"in home"*? Why is it *"sick of* him*"* rather than "sick *from* him"? No logical reason—the expressions are *idiomatic.* Notice in addition that many words take different prepositions to form different idioms. For example to *wait on someone* is different from *to wait for someone.*

Prepositional idioms don't follow rules you can memorize. Fortunately, you don't need rules. You can usually rely on your own ear and your own experience. When you're in doubt about the right preposition for an expression, check a good dictionary. The entry for a word sometimes gives you a phrase showing which preposition to use. When the word is associated with several idioms, they are often listed at the end of the entry. For example, after definitions of *come* in *Webster's New Twentieth Century Dictionary,* you'll find a list of idioms and their meanings: *to come about, to come across, to come along, to come around, to come between,* etc.

Selected list of prepositional idioms

Although far from complete, this list illustrates the importance of prepositions in forming idioms.

accompanied by (in the company of)—The reporter was *accompanied by* his lawyer.

accompanied with (linked with)—Martinez *accompanied* his speech *with* a series of photographs.

accountable for (responsible for)—I am *accountable for* the errors in the book.

accountable to (answerable to someone)—I am *accountable to* the board of directors.

accuse of (*not* with)—He *accused* the speaker *of* lying.

adapt from (a model)—He *adapted* the design *from* one he had seen in Europe.

adapt to (a situation, an environment)—The children soon *adapted to* the new school.

admit of (allow)—The conflict doesn't *admit of* an easy resolution.

admit to, into (a place, a group)—He was *admitted into* the secret organization.

admit to (confess)—Dr. Allan *admitted to* having sent the card.

agree on or upon (something)—We *agreed on* a date for the meeting.

agree to (do something)—We *agree to* pay the damages.

agree with (people, opinions)—The women who were polled *agreed with* the judge.

analogous to (something similar)—Their marriage is *analogous to* a war that no one wins.

angry at (things)—We're *angry at* the lack of attention the proposal received.

angry with (people)—We're *angry with* the people who lied to us about their support.

annoyed at or with (a person)—The doctor was *annoyed at* her nurse for the interruption.

annoyed by (something)—The doctor was *annoyed by* the constant interruptions.

apprehensive for (concerned for)—They are *apprehensive for* the stranded travelers.

apprehensive of (a danger)—The townspeople are *apprehensive of* the approaching storm.

assist at (an event)—He *assisted at* the service.

assist with (someone or something)—Mr. Nguyen *assisted with* the refreshments and the flowers.

based on (*not* in)—The decision was *based on* our experience with the media.

bored by, with (*not* of)—He was *bored by* their speeches and *bored with* his job.

comply with (*not* to)— If you *comply with* the rules, you'll be accepted.

contend for (a position, a prize)—The candidates have *contended for* the office twice.

contend with (an obstacle)—The candidate has to *contend with* his lack of personal charm.

defect in (things)—The *defect in* the system was its inflexibility.

defect of (people, qualities)—A *defect of* conscience caused his action.

depart for (*not* to, a destination)—They *depart for* England tomorrow.

depart from (a destination, a tradition)—They *departed from* their routine today.

differ from (something)—The first version *differs from* the second.

differ with (someone)—I *differ with* you on that issue.

end in (a state, a feeling)—The relationship *ended in* sorrow.

end with (something)—I think the world will *end with* a bang, not a whimper.

enter into (an agreement)—We *entered into* the alliance filled with hope. (Compare *enter* meaning *to go into*, which takes no preposition: We *entered* the room.)

fired from (*not* off of, a job)—He was *fired from* his job on Friday.

grateful for (a benefit)—I am *grateful for* my musical talent.

grateful to (a person)—I am *grateful to* you for the help.

impatient at (a delay)—They were *impatient at* having to wait so long.

impatient for (a result)—We are *impatient for* an answer from the administration.

impatient with (a person)—He was *impatient with* the clerk.

intervene between (the disputants)—I *intervened between* them before they came to blows.

intervene in (a dispute)—I *intervened in* the fight.

invest in (something or someone)—We *invested* our hopes *in* the new leader.

invest with (a quality)—He *invested* her *with* every virtue.

mastery of (a subject)—She demonstrated her *mastery of* mathematics.

mastery over (a person)—She demonstrated her *mastery over* her opponent.

part from (leave)—I *parted from* the group early this year.

part with (a possession)—I *parted with* the Rolls-Royce reluctantly.

reconcile to (an outcome)—They *reconciled* themselves *to* failure.

reconcile with (a person)—He *reconciled with* his parents after they talked.

suspect of (*not* with*)*—I am *suspected of* shoplifting.

true to (form; a person; a belief)—They are *true to* their principles.

true with (an edge, a line)—This metal plate should be *true with* the threshold.

The Cliché

Clichés are trite, overused expressions, many of which rely on figurative language. In the beginning, no expression is a cliché; it's a fresh way of saying something. *Pretty as a picture, old as the hills,* and *smart as a whip* were once, hard as it is to believe, new and exciting comparisons, but through overuse, they've become tiresome, and most writers know enough to avoid them. Notice, however, that less obvious examples turn up frequently in newspapers, in magazines, or on television. For example, someone may be *following his dream,* while someone else may be trying to *burst his bubble.* Sometimes *what you see is what you get,* but other times you meet people who have *a hidden agenda.* Watch out for *real-life superheroes, unsung heroes, human dynamos, living legends,* people who *push the panic button,* people who *live in glass houses,* and even *the man in the street.*

Other types of overused phrases. Along with stale figures of speech are phrases that have been used so often they are clichés: *agonizing reappraisal, contributing factor, first and foremost, grave danger, grieving widow, grisly murder, in the final analysis, integral part, once and for all, one step closer, the be-all and end-all, tried and true, vital role, unforeseen obstacles,* and so on. Faddish words also quickly become overused, so beware of them.

Mixing clichés

A television newswoman described a man as *having signed his own death knell.* Her error illustrates what can happen to a cliché. The newswoman no doubt meant *signed his own death warrant,* an overused expression that means *to cause one's own destruction through a particular act.* But she confused that expression with another, *sounding the death knell,* which means *to announce the end of something,* or, by extension, *to cause the end of something,* as in "Cutting off the funds *sounded the death knell* for the struggling program." Literally, a knell is the sound of a bell ringing slowly, as at a funeral. Obviously, you don't sign a knell.

What happened here was that the newswoman grabbed a familiar phrase and used it without being sure of its meaning or, worse, without caring about its meaning. Clichés invite writers and speakers to use them in what is a *knee-jerk reaction.* Lack of awareness—frequently the villain in bad writing—leads to mistakes. Sometimes the mistakes are funny, as in "He really *gets my dandruff up"* instead of "He really *gets my dander up." (Dander* means *anger or temper,* the expression to *get one's dander up* means to *lose one's temper, become enraged.)*

Avoiding clichés

Before you use any expression or description that sounds familiar to you, think about it carefully. Is there a better way to say what you want to say? Would it be better simply to use literal language than to rely on an expression that is *old hat?* He was *enraged,* rather than he was *hopping mad* or *mad as a wet hen,* for example? But whatever you do, don't use a cliché and then apologize for it, for example, *Pardon my use of the cliché, but it's true that all that glitters is not gold.* The apology does nothing but draw attention to the tired expression.

Using clichés in new ways

Finally, sometimes clichés get new life with a witty turn or a surprising application. For example, the actress Tallulah Bankhead twisted a standard expression when she said, "There is less to this than meets the eye," and H. Rap Brown did it with his line "Violence is as American as cherry pie." If you can use a trite expression or cliché in a new, surprising way, you are overcoming the predictability that is its *stock in trade.* But, as with all attempts at cleverness, be sure that you're achieving the effect you want and not just making a bad joke.

Jargon

One definition of **jargon** is that it is the specialized language of a particular field or profession—psychology, sociology, economics, literature, mathematics, biology, anthropology, and so on. When you are writing a paper in a particular field, you can use the specialized terms that are accepted and understood in that field. In fact, you will probably have to.

Negative connotations of jargon

The term *jargon* has other, less neutral definitions, and the connotations of the term are almost always negative. Jargon can seem like gibberish, language unintelligible to most people. When a special term arises because it describes or explains or categorizes something in a helpful way, it is acceptable, but when jargon becomes a way of making something sound more scientific or complex than it really is, it should be avoided. Jargon is sometimes merely doubletalk and is also often responsible for wordy, heavy-handed sentences.

Avoiding jargon

In your writing, avoid using specialized terms from a particular field unless you are writing in or about that field. For example, you can talk about *computers interfacing* more appropriately than about *people interfacing*. *Risk-averse investments* is a tolerable phrase; *risk-averse children* should be changed to *children who are afraid to take risks.* Don't use a specialized term like *paranoia,* which in psychiatry is a mental disorder characterized by delusions, to describe people's lack of ease around strangers or a parent's nervousness about a child. Be careful of scientific terms *(critical constants, entropy, genotype, etc.).* These specialized terms have distinct meanings, and if you borrow them to describe other phenomena, you may be making a mistake. At the very least, you may confuse your reader.

Faddish Words

Faddish words are words that you suddenly see and hear everywhere. Commentators, advertisers, public relations people, educators, business people, and so on pick up or coin terms that then enjoy a moment (or longer) in the sun: *dysfunctional, parenting, syndrome, ethnicity, decision-making, cultural diversity, dialogue* (as a *verb*), *viable, counterproductive, entrepreneurial,* etc. Some of them last, some fade, some disappear altogether. Faddish words can quickly become overused expressions.

Slang

Most people who write formal reports and essays avoid **slang**, which is usually an appropriate thing to do. In an analysis of post-Cold-War Russia, it would be inappropriate, for example, to talk about *heavy-duty* problems or describe the situation as *the pits.* Writing about the injuries of accident victims, you wouldn't say *they grossed me out* or that the paramedics' response was *totally awesome,* even though you might use expressions like these when talking to a friend.

Sometimes slang can be used in writing, however. In dialogue, it can quickly characterize a speaker. In a humorous piece, a slang word like *freak* (as in *neatness freak)* might work. Remember, though, that slang words lose their vigor and quickly become outdated—the *cat's pajamas, keen, swell, hip, groovy,* etc. As with all language, when you use slang, know what you are doing and why you are doing it.

The Euphemism

A **euphemism** is a mild or roundabout word or phrase used in place of one considered painful or offensive—for example, *golden years* for *old age* or *economically disadvantaged* for *poor.* Other kinds of euphemisms, rather than covering up, inflate or magnify, making something sound more important or grander than it is: *technical representative* for *salesperson,* for example, or *handcrafted* for *handmade.*

People use euphemisms to protect themselves and others from the hard facts of life—for example, *senior citizen* for *old person, discomfort* for *pain, pass away* for *die.* People also use euphemisms like *sleeping together, having a relationship,* or *going to the bathroom* to be polite. In social settings, euphemisms like these can be justified as preserving the amenities.

But people use euphemisms for dangerous reasons too—to cover up or prettify motives and events. For example, the phrase *a strategic movement to the rear* sounds less humiliating than *retreat.* A *preemptive strike* is much more acceptable than a *sneak attack.* Politicians *misspeak* themselves rather than make gross errors of fact, or they describe previous statements as *currently inoperative* rather than admit that they *lied.* Corporate executives *restructure* or *downsize* rather than *lay off* or *fire* employees. The euphemism *human resource department* for what used to be a personnel department attempts to humanize the people who have to deal firsthand with firing employees. Perhaps it is also intended to persuade employees that the business sees them as people, not just personnel. Public relations professionals (a euphemistic job title for those who project a sympathetic image for institutions and individuals willing to pay them) come up with creative ways to make something sound better (or less bad) than it is.

Euphemisms and **doubletalk** are closely related. A phrase in doubletalk, like a euphemism, is a roundabout way of saying something. It can be hard to figure out what a statement in doubletalk means, which is what its originators had in mind. Often more sinister than a euphemism, doubletalk is almost always intended to confuse or deceive.

Avoiding euphemisms

Socially, you may need to use some euphemisms if you don't want to be ostracized or thought insensitive. In your writing, however, strive to be direct. Beware the temptation to be overly polite, to cover up hard facts, or to inflate something by using a euphemistic term. Question euphemisms and doubletalk statements created by others; don't perpetuate them in your own writing. You should communicate to your readers not only as clearly but also as truthfully as you can.

Selected list of euphemisms

Euphemisms are everywhere, and more are born each day. This brief list should make you think about the various reasons they exist.

au naturel: naked

categorical inaccuracy: lie

character line: wrinkle

clarify: sometimes used euphemistically to mean one is retracting a previous statement

collateral damage: in a bombing, civilian casualties and destruction of civilian buildings

comfort station: public toilet

correctional facility: prison

(the) departed: the dead person; died

direct mail: unsolicited mail; junk mail

disincentive: penalty; reprisal

disinformation: lie

electronic surveillance: wiretapping and bugging

ethnic cleansing: eliminating people from racial or national backgrounds different from your own; *eliminating* is itself a euphemism for deporting, or killing

expecting: pregnant

fabricate: make up

freedom fighters: rebels fighting a government seen as hostile to one's own interests

friendly fire: artillery fire from one's own forces that accidentally or mistakenly wounds or kills someone on one's own side

funeral director: an undertaker

furlough (employees): lay off

happy hour: time set aside for drinking, usually in late afternoon

honorarium: payment

imbibe: drink

indisposed: ill (being)

intimate: having sexual intercourse

inventory leakage: theft

job action: a strike or work slow-down

landfill: garbage or garbage dump

message: commercial: a message from our sponsor

mobile home: trailer

negative patient care outcome: the patient died

neutralize: to take out of action, to kill

out-placement: help from the company that fired you to find a new job

out-source: for cost-saving purposes, to farm out work to outside workers to whom no benefits need be paid rather than hire full-time workers with benefits

pacify: to repress or destroy an enemy

personal flotation device: life preserver on an airplane

personal representative: salesperson

position: job

preowned: used, for example, used car

relocation center: an American-style prison camp used to hold Japanese-Americans during World War II

remains: dead body

revenue enhancements: taxes

reverse engineering: taking something apart to see how it works and then copying it

stress-producing stimulus: electric shock

surreptitious entry: break-in

therapeutic misadventure: surgeon's error

visually challenged: blind, *challenged* has become part of a host of euphemisms both serious and humorous (for example, *chronologically challenged* for *old*)

Chapter Checkout

Q&A

1. Choose the correct idiom to complete the following sentences.
   a. Carlos was reconciled to/with the biologist, who was his mentor.
   b. Ryan agreed on/to/with sharing the cost of the vacation.
   c. Clearly frustrated, the swimmer was annoyed at/by the judge's scores.

2. Do the following sentences contain an example of either jargon, faddish words, or slang? Answer yes or no.
   a. It's cool to wear those colors this year.
   b. My hard drive crashed last night because the graphics card was overloaded.
   c. The results of her findings will have long lasting repercussions throughout the psychiatric community.

3. Underline the cliché in the following sentences.
   a. The weight lifter was as strong as an ox.
   b. Sharp as a tack, Rosita never lost at chess.
   c. After the initial questions, the inquest was smooth sailing for him.

4. Match the euphemism to its corresponding word.
   a. position   incorrect
   b. disincentive   move
   c. downsizing   job
   d. pass away   penalty
   e. imbibe   die
   f. relocation   lay off / fire
   g. misinformed   drink

Answers: 1. a. with b. to c. by 2. a. yes b. yes c. no 3. a. strong as an ox b. sharp as a tack c. smooth sailing 4. a. job b. penalty c. lay off/fire d. die e. drink f. move g. incorrect.

Chapter 12

COMPOUND WORDS
AND WORDINESS

Chapter Check-In

❑ Mastering compound words

❑ Using too many words

❑ Avoiding redundancy

Effective writing requires more than just correct vocabulary. You must also spell words correctly. Most word processing software has a spelling correction feature, but you should also invest in a good dictionary to reduce spelling mistakes and find word definitions.

Be aware of the impact of the words you choose. Words have specific meanings and should not be repeated without a good reason. Unnecessary or repeated words and phrases make writing seem cluttered. You can avoid wordiness by using the active voice, which is a more direct way to phrase your sentences. Proper spelling and careful word choice are essential ingredients for good writing.

Spelling of Compound Words

Compound words are a spelling problem, not a vocabulary problem; to hyphenate or not to hyphenate is usually the issue. Unfortunately, there's no simple answer. Compound words are sometimes spelled solid *(halfback, oversight, torchbearer, halfhearted, midweek),* sometimes written as separate words *(top hat, decision maker, reddish orange),* and sometimes hyphenated *(half-moon, self-knowledge, one-half, able-bodied).* Also, over time some words lose their hyphens and are spelled solid. Some rules apply, but there are too many to memorize, with too many exceptions. For example, while *wagon train* and *pool table* are each written as two words, *wagonload* and *poolroom* are each written as one, with no rule to explain the difference.

The best thing to do when you aren't sure is to consult an unabridged dictionary. If the compound is a noun, you have a good chance of finding it. If it's an adjective, your chances are fair. If you can't find the word you're looking for, you can try applying some general principles.

Current trend in spelling compound words

The current trend is away from hyphens, as in *handshake, notebook, taxpayer, poolroom, crosswalk,* etc. When a compound is temporary (that is, used for a particular purpose or not in the dictionary), you can either hyphenate it or spell it as two words: *quasi-normal, pool cover.*

Compound adjectives

Many, but not all, **compound adjectives** are hyphenated when they appear before nouns *(cross-country trip, full-length mirror, half-baked scheme* but *midweek meeting, worldwide circulation, halfhearted support).* Again, check your dictionary. When a compound adjective is temporary and not in the dictionary, it is customary to hyphenate it: *horseshoe-shaped driveway, top-ranked athlete, velvet-trimmed coat.* Using a hyphen is especially important if the compound adjective could mislead a reader. For example, *fast-moving van* means a van that is going fast, whereas *fast moving van* means a moving van that is going fast.

When a compound adjective *follows* a noun, the hyphen is omitted: The athlete was *top ranked;* The driveway was *horseshoe shaped;* The coat was *velvet trimmed;* The van was *fast moving.*

Compound adverbs

While most **compound adverbs** are written as two words *(distributed all over, going full speed),* those adverbial compounds beginning with *over* or *under* are spelled solid *(overeagerly, underhandedly).* Adverbial compounds consisting of spelled-out fractions are hyphenated: *two-thirds completed.*

Words with Prefixes and Suffixes

Today, words with prefixes and suffixes, with a few exceptions, are spelled solid whether they are nouns, verbs, adjectives, or adverbs. Among the most common prefixes and suffixes are *anti (antiwar), bi (bilingual), co (coauthor), counter (counterclockwise), extra (extrasensory), inter (internecine), intra (intramural), mid (midlevel), mini (minivan), multi (multimedia), neo (neorealism), non (nonbeliever), over (override), post (postwar), pre (prefabricated), pseudo (pseudoscientific), re (reexamine), semi (semiconductor), sub (substandard), trans (transatlantic), un (unexamined),* and *under (undervalued).*

You can make exceptions to this trend. Check a dictionary first, and, if the word is not there, it is customary to use a hyphen in these situations.

- The second element is capitalized: *anti-British, mid-Victorian* (BUT *transatlantic*).

- There might be confusion with another word: *recover* vs. *re-cover.*

- The second element consists of more than one word: *non-church-attending.*

- The prefix ends with the same letter that begins the root word: *anti-intellectual* (but *reenter, reexamine*).

- The combination creates an odd or confusing form that could be misread *(pro-life* vs. *prolife*).

Wordy Expressions

A redundant expression says the same thing twice, and doubletalk avoids getting directly to the point. Both are examples of wordy expressions. Other such expressions use more than one word when one will do—for example, *in the vicinity of* instead of *near*—not necessarily to mislead or cover up but because a writer is careless or afraid to write simply.

Redundant expressions

In writing, **redundancy** means conveying the same meaning twice. Like other kinds of wordiness, redundancy makes writing fat. Sometimes people use redundant expressions because they don't recognize the precise definition of a word. For example, *close proximity* is redundant because *proximity* by itself means *nearness.* Can there be any other kind of nearness than close nearness? Other times people fall into redundant expressions because they don't pay enough attention to what they are writing—for example, *small in size, few in number,* or *red in color.*

Selected list of redundant expressions

Look for redundant expressions and you'll find them easily. Tables 12-1 and 12-2 present a short list to get you started. When you write, check your drafts to make sure you are getting the full value of the words you choose and not adding unnecessary ones.

Table 12-1   Adjectives, Adverbs, Nouns

advance warning	free gift	sad lament
advance planning	fundamental basis	same identical
close intimates	future ahead	sudden impulse
close scrutiny	human artifact	true fact
completely unanimous	Jewish rabbi	tuna fish
consensus of opinion	more better	two opposites
currently at this time	new innovation	unexpected surprise
empty void	now pending	unimportant triviality
end result	past history	wealthy millionaire
exact same	present incumbent	yearly annual
famous celebrity	rejected outcast	

Table 12-2   Verbs

advance forward	leave from	retreat back
continue on	lower down	return back
cooperate together	proceed forward	share in common
enter into (buildings)	raise up	share together
join together	retract back	

There is, there are, it is **expressions**

Many wordy expressions make use of *there is, there are,* or *it is.* These constructions can often be eliminated.

> *There is* a famous author who lives on my block.
>
> BETTER   A famous author lives on my block.
>
> *There are* many people who like television.
>
> BETTER   Many people like television.
>
> *There are* some animals that thrive in arctic temperatures.
>
> BETTER   Some animals thrive in arctic temperatures.
>
> *It is* rarely *the case that* people refuse to help.
>
> BETTER   People rarely refuse to help.
>
> *It is a fact that* most of us like to be praised.
>
> BETTER   Most of us like to be praised.

Overused intensifiers

Intensifiers are words intended to add force to what you say: *very, absolutely, positively, really, quite,* and so on. Sometimes you need them, but more often you can prune them without it affecting your tone or meaning. Review the following examples.

> Roosevelt, *certainly a quite active president,* refused to give in to his handicap.

BETTER   Roosevelt, *an active president,* refused to give in to his handicap.

> She *positively expects* to win this election.

BETTER   She *expects* to win this election.

> The results were *very surprising.*

BETTER   The results were *surprising.*

Selected list of wordy expressions

Thousands of wordy expressions exist, and new ones are created every day. Following are a few examples. Check your writing for similar roundabout ways of saying something.

after the conclusion of = **after:** *After* the concert we left NOT *After the conclusion of* the concert we left.

all of = **all:** *All* the boys came NOT *All of* the boys came.

any and all = **any or all:** We appreciate *any* suggestions NOT We appreciate *any and all* suggestions.

at the present moment, at this point in time = **now:** We are looking for a solution *now* NOT We are looking for a solution *at the present moment.*

by means of = **by:** He came *by* car NOT He came *by means* of a car.

due to the fact that = **because:** *Because* he called, we waited NOT *Due to the fact that* he called, we waited.

for the purpose of (+ gerund) = **to:** The meeting is *to* discuss plans NOT The meeting is *for the purpose of* discussing plans.

for the simple reason that = **because:** She won *because* she was best NOT She won *for the simple reason that* she was best.

he is a man who is = **he is:** *He is* admired NOT *He is a man who* is admired.

in a place where = **where:** They lived *where* no trees grew NOT They lived *in a place where* no trees grew.

in connection with = about: He telephoned *about* the rally NOT He telephoned *in connection with* the rally.

in order to = to: He said this *to* help you NOT He said this *in order to* help you.

in spite of the fact that = although or though: *Although* she agreed, she was sad NOT *In spite of the fact that* she agreed, she was sad.

in the near future = soon: We'll see you *soon* NOT We'll see you *in the near future.*

in view of the fact that = because: *Because* she helped us, we won NOT *In view of the fact that* she helped us, we won.

is located in = is in: Ventura County *is in* California NOT Ventura County *is located in* California.

it often happens that = often: *Often* he is invited to attend NOT *It often happens that* he is invited to attend.

on the part of = by: A suggestion *by* the consultant helped NOT A suggestion *on the part of* the consultant helped.

owing to the fact that = because: *Because* he was here, we stayed NOT *Owing to the fact* that he was here, we stayed.

practice in the field of = practice: She *practices* medicine NOT She *practices in the field of* medicine.

rarely ever = rarely: She *rarely* speaks to a large group NOT She *rarely ever* speaks to a large group.

the fact is that, the truth is that = often omit altogether: You are the right candidate NOT *The fact is that* you are the right candidate.

which was when = when: I spoke with him yesterday *when* he called NOT I spoke with him yesterday, *which was when* he called.

with the exception of = except: I like all sports *except* boxing NOT I like all sports *with the exception of* boxing.

Active Voice vs. Passive Voice

Reduce wordiness by using the active voice rather than the passive voice of the verb whenever you can (see Chapter 2). The active voice is not only more energetic but also more concise. Look at the following examples of weak passives:

> The windows *had been smashed by* the wind sometime during the night.

BETTER The wind *smashed* the windows sometime during the night.

A speech *was given* by the delegate from Michigan, and a challenge *was issued* by him to everyone attending.

BETTER   The delegate from Michigan gave a speech and *issued* a challenge to everyone attending.

After the town *was hit* by a tornado, a call to the Red Cross *was made* by our mayor.

BETTER   After a tornado *hit* the town, our mayor *called* the Red Cross.

Chapter Checkout

Q&A

1. True or False: All of the following underlined compound words are spelt correctly.
   a. The Oceanic Restaurant is <u>worldfamous</u> for their crab dip.
   b. The <u>poolroom</u> was brightly lit.
   c. Their <u>long-distance</u> relationship ended abruptly.
   d. Mercy Hospital specializes in <u>neonatal</u> care.

2. True or False: The following statements are wordy.
   a. Jess Luna is the man who ran for President.
   b. There are several good reasons why you should visit Prague.
   c. We stayed home because of the fact that Theresa was ill.
   d. There are several guests arriving late.

3. Match the wordy expression to its simpler complement. You may use one complement more than once.
   a. By means of   because
   b. In the very near future   except
   c. Due to the fact that   now
   d. As a result of   by
   e. At the current time   soon
   f. With the lone exception of
   g. In consideration of

Answers: 1 a. False b. True c. True d. True 2. *a.* True b. False c. True d. True 3. a. by b. soon c. because d. because e. now f. except g. because.

Chapter 13

PREWRITING: HOW TO BEGIN A WRITING ASSIGNMENT

Chapter Check-In

❏ Defining the writing process

❏ Determining your audience

❏ Selecting a topic

❏ Creating a thesis

Writing is a process. The formula good writers follow consists of prewriting, writing, and rewriting, or revising and editing. This allows their work to emerge in a series of small manageable steps.

Your main purpose in writing is to inform, persuade, or entertain. Defining your purpose or goal is the first step. Select a topic that is narrow enough to be explained within your page limitations. A thesis, unlike a topic, is a single statement that makes an assertion about a topic. It is usually placed somewhere in the introduction of an essay. Often, a thesis sentence will give the reader a clear overview of the essay by stating the main ideas. Generally, if you choose a topic that is interesting to you, then your reader will find it interesting too.

The Steps in Writing

Although it is a process, writing doesn't progress as neatly from one step to the next as does, for example, baking a cake or changing a tire. Roughly speaking, when you write you

■ Decide on a topic (or have a topic assigned to you)

■ Explore ideas about the topic through thinking, reading, listening, and so on

- Formulate a thesis or main idea and decide what points you want to make to support it

- Select details and examples (from reading, research, personal experience)

- Decide on the order in which you'll present your ideas and examples

- Write a first draft; edit and revise for content, style, and writing mechanics; write a final draft

At any time during this process, you may need to stop and go back several steps. For example, when you're selecting details and examples, you may realize your topic is too broad or your thesis statement weak. Or when you're organizing your points, you may see that the thesis you *thought* you were developing isn't the one that you *are* developing. Often the act of writing itself generates new ideas you may want to pursue. Even as late as your final draft you may decide that the organization isn't working, or you may spot a flaw in your argument that causes you to throw out much of what you've written and rework the rest. The most realistic way to view writing is not as a straight line but as a back-and-forward movement. Take that into account when deciding how long you'll need to finish a writing assignment.

Types of Writing

The writing you're required to do in your lifetime varies—for example, timed writings and essay questions on exams; autobiographical essays for college applications; high-school and college papers on a variety of subjects; business letters, proposals, and reports related to your work. In most of your writing you'll be doing one of the following:

- Describing a person, place, or thing

- Telling a story or recounting an incident

- Reporting information

- Providing instructions or explaining a process

- Arguing a position or proving a point

- Analyzing something—a text, a theory, an attitude, or an event

The techniques you use will overlap. For example, if you're writing a descriptive essay about your Aunt Gladys, you might narrate an incident that reveals her personality.

Most—though not all—college writing assignments focus on argument and analysis. But within an essay arguing a position, you might use descriptive and narrative techniques. In a paper taking a stand against capital punishment, you might include a vivid description of a gas chamber, or recount the steps of an execution, or even narrate an incident. In choosing your approach to any writing task, be guided by your purpose and the best way to fulfill it.

Understanding Your Assignment

If you're given a writing assignment, fulfilling it is your main purpose. Understand what you are asked to do. In an examination question, for example, if you're asked to analyze how an author's techniques contribute to his theme, and if you describe the theme thoroughly but don't discuss the techniques, then you've failed to fulfill the assignment. Or if in a psychology class you're asked to compare and contrast two recent theories about selective amnesia, and you write five pages on one of the theories and only half a page on the other, you probably haven't done what is required.

Writing on the job is no different. For example, if you need to write a testing protocol for a new product, you should include such things as a detailed description of the testing samples and the control group, the conditions of testing, materials and equipment, all the steps of the tests, relevant formulas and equations, and the methods to be used in evaluating results. If after the testing your manager asks for a summary of the results, you should provide them as clearly, honestly, and succinctly as you can. You may need to include a brief explanation of the tests, but you won't want to give a blow-by-blow account.

Whether you're writing in school or at work, make sure that you understand your task. Then, in planning what you'll write, aim everything you say at achieving that purpose.

Understanding Your Audience

For whom are you writing? Before you begin, think about your **audience.** A reader is at the other end of your writing, and you should keep that reader in mind.

Student writers sometimes think that their audience is a stuffy instructor who will be impressed by big words and long sentences. But most teachers know good, clear writing when they see it. Most can distinguish between solid content and inflated trivia. If you have little to say but dress it up in overblown prose with commas in all the right places, you won't fare as well as someone who has something to say and says it clearly, even with a few mechanical errors.

The reason you're writing and the audience you're writing for are closely related, so be realistic. If you're writing a letter to a surfing magazine praising a new board, you'll use different language and a different tone than you will in a college paper on Mikhail Gorbachev's success in attempting to modernize Russia in the late 1980s. Though both audiences want to understand and be interested in what you write, they'll expect and respond to different styles. Changing your language, style, or tone to meet specific circumstances is fine. But don't make the mistake of thinking that you can be straightforward in the letter to the surfing magazine while you should strive to sound important in the paper on Gorbachev.

Ask yourself some specific questions about your audience before you begin. Among some things to consider

- **Are you writing for people in a particular field, such as psychology, English literature, or genetics?** Can you assume knowledge of the terminology and concepts you'll be using, or do you need to define them in the paper? Will you need to provide extensive background information on the subject you plan to discuss, or will a brief summary be enough?

- **What expectations does your audience have?** An audience of marine biologists will have different expectations from an article on marine biology than will a general audience, for example.

- **Are you writing for someone who insists on certain writing practices or who has pet peeves?** One instructor may require a five-paragraph essay, or another may forbid the use of intentional sentence fragments. Be aware of any requirements or restrictions. On grammar, punctuation, and usage questions, if you aren't sure about a particular instructor, you're safest taking a conservative path.

- **What is the reading level of your audience?** Instructions and explanations written for fourth graders shouldn't include college-level vocabulary, for example.

■ **Are you writing for an audience that is likely to agree or disagree with your point of view?** Consider this question if you're writing an argumentative or editorial piece. It can make a difference in the language you select, the amount of proof you offer, and the tone you use. An editorial for a small-town paper on the importance of family values, for example, is less likely to encounter resistance from the audience than an editorial on legalizing drugs.

Guidelines for Choosing a Topic

Often you're assigned a topic to write about or asked to choose among several. When you must create your own, keep in mind these points.

■ **Choose a topic appropriate to the length of your paper.** Generally, students pick topics that are too broad to be adequately covered. Narrow topics lead to close observation, while broad topics lead to generalizations and sketchy development. If you're writing a five-page paper, don't write on the history of women's rights; instead, write about one incident in the history of women's rights. Even a personal or descriptive essay will be better if you choose a narrow topic—my childhood in a small town, for example, rather than my childhood, or my uncle's barn, rather than the Midwest.

■ **Avoid a topic that will tempt you to summarize rather than to discuss or analyze.** Don't choose *the plot of Macbeth* but *how the final scene of Macbeth illustrates the play's theme.* The second topic is narrower and less likely to lead to summary. When considering a topic, ask yourself if it can lead to a reasonable thesis.

■ **Choose a topic that interests you.** If you don't care about limiting cigarette advertising, don't select it as a topic for a persuasive essay. You'll have more to say and write better on something you care about.

■ **If your assignment requires research, choose a topic on which you can find material.** Even when you aren't writing a research paper, make sure that you've picked a subject that you can develop with sufficient details.

■ **After you've picked a topic, don't be afraid to change it if it isn't working out.** Instructors would rather you write a good essay than that you grind out pages on something you realize was a bad choice.

Topic vs. thesis

Don't confuse a topic with a main idea or thesis. The topic provides the subject; the thesis makes an assertion about that subject. Here are a few examples of topics that might be assigned to a college student:

> Compare and contrast X's poem *"To a Wolf"* with Y's poem *"The Happy Meercat."* Consider both theme and technique.

> Discuss the following statement: "No matter how much we may deplore human rights violations in China, the United States should not impose sanctions on the Chinese government." Do you agree or disagree? Support your opinion.

> Analyze Shakespeare's use of clothing imagery in *King Lear.*

> Describe an incident in your life that caused you to change an opinion or attitude.

> "The Civil War had much more to do with economics than with morality." Do you agree or disagree with this statement? Support your opinion.

Two of these topics (the second and fifth) ask the writer to argue a position. A sentence expressing that position is a **thesis** statement. A thesis statement for the second topic might be, *Imposing sanctions on China would be a mistake because it would hurt the American economy, because sanctions are notoriously unsuccessful as a way to force change, and because the United States should not interfere in the internal policies of other countries.*

While the remaining three topics don't ask the writer to take a position, for a good essay on any of these topics, the writer should formulate a thesis. A thesis statement for the first might be, *Although both poet X and poet Y show appreciation for their subjects, poet X's Wolf symbolizes the separation between humans and other animals, while poet Y's Meercat symbolizes the connection between all living things.* With this thesis statement, the writer makes a point about the topic and sets up a direction for the essay.

Writing a thesis statement

Whenever you write a paper analyzing, discussing, comparing, identifying causes or effects, or arguing a position, you should be able to write a thesis statement. You can refine and improve it as you go along, but try to begin with a one-sentence statement. A thesis statement can help you steer a straight course, avoiding the danger of digression.

Make your thesis statement say something. Don't be satisfied with weak generalities that fail to zero in on your main point. The following are examples of pseudo-thesis statements:

> Poets X and Y make important points about animals in their poems *"To a Wolf"* and *"The Happy Meercat."*

> People hold different opinions as to whether it is wise to impose sanctions on China because of their human rights violations.

> Shakespeare uses quite a bit of clothing imagery in *King Lear.*

None of these statements provides a clear direction for an essay because the assertions they make are so vague, they are useless. A better thesis statement for the third example might be, *Clothing images in King Lear reflect the development of Lear from a man blinded by appearances to a man able to face the naked truth.* Remember that the creation of a thesis statement is important to the way you approach your topic, helping you direct your thinking as well as your writing.

Avoiding fallacies

As you write be careful to avoid logic fallacies and ideological reasoning. *Logic fallacies* are problems in thinking or connecting ideas. Common fallacies include:

- **Ad Hominem:** Also called name-calling, this fallacy is an attack either directly or indirectly on a person.

  > Bob can't be right because he is an idiot.

- **Bandwagon/Celebrity Appeal:** This is a fallacy that implies the reader should agree with a premise because a majority or a particularly significant person agrees with the premise.

  > As everyone knows, this bill will help our children.

- **Either/Or Reasoning:** Assuming that there can be only one cause or one solution in an issue.

  > The only way to keep our children safe is to ban video games.

- **Slippery Slope:** Assuming that because one minor fact is true, then a larger premise must be too, despite any further proof.

  > Congressman Smith voted against tax increases last week; therefore, Congressman Smith will always be against tax increases.

- **Ad Populum:** Arguing based upon emotional appeals rather than facts.

  All true Americans want to ban this book.

- **Circular Reasoning:** Presents as reasons a restatement of the problem.

  There are not enough parking spaces because there are too many cars.

Ideological reasoning is the use of cultural, religious, or moral values and beliefs to prove a position. While there is nothing wrong with making personal judgments in this way, you should always be aware that your audience might not share your ideological views. To reach the greatest number of individuals you should avoid making ideological reasons the foundation of your arguments.

The Main Idea in Narratives and Personal Essays

Narrative and personal essays also require a main or controlling idea to help you focus and direct your writing. For example, consider this topic: *Describe an incident in your life that caused you to change an opinion or attitude.* Before you begin writing, create a sentence that will both identify the incident you plan to narrate and describe the change it caused. Below are some examples of main idea statements.

The divorce of my parents when I was seven changed my view that adults were infallible and always in control of their own lives.

When I was six, my cat Edward died; and I began to mistrust the reassurances of doctors, a mistrust that has remained with me ever since.

Changing high schools when I was fifteen made me realize for the first time that the fear of an experience is often worse than the reality.

When you write your paper, you may decide to suggest your main idea indirectly rather than state it. But making yourself create a statement is still a good idea.

Chapter Checkout

Q&A

1. Identify the potential problems with the following thesis statements.
   a. World religions are remarkably similar.
   b. Gun Control is the only way to stop violence in schools.
   c. The invention of the television destroyed the American family.
   d. Brad should not be president of the garden club because he is a jerk.
   e. Rock music is bad because it is against my religion.

2. Identify the following as Topic TP or Thesis TH.
   a. Medieval harp music performed in Italy
   b. Aids research on patients who were diagnosed before 1985
   c. Smoking should be banned in public places.
   d. Aids funding is insufficient to meet the needs of researchers.

3. True or False: All of the following statements about writing are true.
   a. Writing is a process.
   b. All writing is done for one purpose.
   c. Audience is important in writing.
   d. Topics should be chosen based upon what impresses teachers.
   e. A thesis is a topic spelled out in a full sentence.
   f. A thesis should never be based on logic fallacies.

Answers: 1. a. Unless you are writing a book, this topic is too broad b. This is a fallacy because it assumes that there is only one solution. c. This is a fallacy because it assumes that the one event caused another simply because of chronological order. d. This is a fallacy because it is name-calling. e. This is a fallacy because it argues from an ideological position that all readers may not share. 2 a. TP b. TP c. TH d. TH. 3 a. True b. False c. True d. False e. False f. True.

Chapter 14

PREWRITING: HOW TO RESEARCH AND ORGANIZE

Chapter Check-In

❑ Researching effectively

❑ Organizing ideas to support a thesis

❑ Planning the essay

Once you have narrowed your topic and established a working thesis, you can start researching your essay. You may want to begin by writing what you know about the topic before you head to the library or the Internet. Generally, information that is assumed to be common knowledge does not have to be identified. However, you should identify, either by quote or citation, all specific phrasing that comes from another writer. Paraphrasing is a valuable way to summarize long passages or ideas from other writers.

Write an outline to focus and develop the main ideas that support or explain your thesis. You can organize your ideas in a variety of spatial or chronological ways. If you make your outline detailed, then the body of the essay should be easy to write. While a written outline can seem like extra work, it is a valuable, almost essential, key to writing a good first draft.

Finding Examples and Evidence

When you have a topic, you begin thinking of what you'll say. Write a thesis statement to organize your thinking. Before you start writing, take notes. For personal essays, write down your thoughts, observations, memories, and experiences. When analyzing a text, take notes on the significant sections or underline them. For most other essays, read materials with an eye to finding details, examples, and illustrations to support your main idea.

If you want to use quotations, write them down accurately. Remember that you'll need to footnote tiny facts, ideas, or quotations you borrow from other sources, so be sure to include bibliographical information in your notes. Some of what you write down will probably never appear in your essay. Your notes might even include questions that occur to you as you read, possibilities you want to explore, warnings to yourself, or reminders to check further on certain points. This stage of preparing a paper is not only to ensure that you have examples and evidence but also to help you think in more detail about your topic and thesis.

Brainstorming, taking notes, and outlining

Begin the process by trying freewriting on the computer. You can get ideas down quickly and legibly and save them as a brainstorming file; later, you can import parts of this file into your first draft. Take notes on the computer too, being sure to include the information you'll need to cite references. Word-processing programs can format and place footnotes when you're at the point of preparing your final draft, but of course you are responsible for accurately recording the sources of your information. If your writing project requires a bibliography, start a list of your references. Later you can easily add to and rearrange the list.

Most programs have a feature that allows you to create a formal outline according to a style you choose, such as roman numerals for headings, alpha characters for first-level subheadings, and so on. If you go back into your outline to add a heading or subheading, the program will automatically update your outline designations. Changing an outline on your computer is so simple that you can experiment with different organizational plans.

Using the computer for research

With a computer, you can gain access to thousands of documents and databases, some in portable form on CD-ROMs (disks that store large amounts of information) and some directly online. You can call up journal and newspaper articles, abstracts, a variety of encyclopedias and dictionaries, and much more. Through the Internet (which includes the World Wide Web), you can view databases on many subjects and have access to library archival materials. The challenge is to know what there is and how to search for it. So much information is available online that you may feel overwhelmed and frustrated. Before you use the Internet to do serious research, it's a good idea to get some training. How-to books and classes are available, as are Internet directories that steer you in the right direction. Once you are online, search systems (or search engines)—to which you enter key words—help you navigate. When you use information from electronic sources in a paper, consult a current style guide (such as the *MLA Handbook for Writers of Research Papers,* Fourth Edition) on the correct forms for citing it in footnotes and a bibliography.

The Importance of Specific Details

A frequent mistake in writing is failing to provide specific examples, evidence, or details to support an idea or thesis. In an essay about a poem, for example, it isn't enough to say that the author's language creates a dark, gloomy atmosphere; you must cite particular words and images that demonstrate this effect. In an essay arguing that magnet schools in cities improve education for minority students, you must provide some evidence—statistics, anecdotes, and so on. In a timed writing on the statement, *We learn more from our failures than our successes,* you shouldn't merely reflect on the statement; you should cite examples from your life, or from the news, or from history.

Remember that essays filled with general unsupported statements are not only unconvincing, but also uninteresting.

Plagiarism

As you take notes, be aware that when you write your paper you must cite any sources you use, so record the information you'll need for footnotes. Consult a style guide for proper footnoting and preparation of a bibliography. You'll be guilty of **plagiarism** if you don't properly give credit for words or ideas that you borrow from others.

Most people understand that they can't steal exact words from a source, but some believe that paraphrasing—simply borrowing an idea—is acceptable. Generally, it isn't. While you don't need to footnote well-known ideas such as evolution or easily accessible facts such as the date of the first moon landing, you should document less generally known ideas or opinions (for example, a news analyst's assessment of a Supreme Court decision), and less accessible facts (such as the number of motorcycles sold in the United States in a given year). Deciding what to footnote is sometimes a gray area, but play it safe. If you have doubts, cite your source.

Quoting and paraphrasing

When should you use quotations in a paper, and when should you paraphrase information instead? If you want to make a point about an author's language or style,—as in the analysis of a literary work—use quotations.

But don't quote an entire stanza if you are going to comment on only two words, and don't give up your responsibility to discuss a character simply by quoting a descriptive passage from a novel.

If your interest is in the information a source conveys rather than in the author's expression, consider paraphrasing (putting the information in your own words) rather than quoting, particularly if the relevant passage is long and includes material you don't need. The question to ask is, "Why am I choosing to include this quotation?" If you have a good reason—an author's language or tone, for example, or a particularly apt expression— go ahead. But often you're after only the information or part of the information.

Consider the following passage:

> Community-based policing has given rise to several important questions, among them the following: Should police officers address social problems that extend beyond particular crimes? Some experts on police reform say yes, while others say no. Although there is agreement that having police officers walk regular beats can decrease community suspicion and deter lawbreakers, the experts who are against greater involvement feel that giving police a broader responibility by expecting them to deal with problems such as urban decay and irresponsible parenting is unrealistic and ultimately undesirable.

If you're writing about attitudes towards police reform, why not paraphrase the point that relates to your topic as shown in the following paragraph?

> Police-reform experts disagree about many issues, including whether or not police should involve themselves in social issues that go beyond their direct responsibility to deter crime and apprehend lawbreakers.

Don't pad a paper with quotations to add to its length (you'll irritate the instructor) and don't quote heavily to prove that you've read a source and have evidence for your points. Paraphrasing works just as well. One caution, however. Paraphrasing a source requires correct citation (footnoting) just as quotation does.

The Writing Assignment

All assignments are not identical, and you can use different strategies as you approach each writing task. The main purpose of your project may be research, argument, analysis, or narrative. In each of these areas you can learn some basic skills that will make the work easier.

The research paper

Don't regard a research paper as unlike other writing assignments. As in other essays, you should have a topic, a thesis, an introduction, good organization, unified and coherent paragraphs, transitions, and so on. A research paper should *not* consist of footnoted facts loosely strung together.

However, unlike other essays, a research paper depends on the use and citation of several sources of information, such as reference books, books related to your subject, relevant journal and magazine articles, speeches, and lectures. During the information-gathering period, get to know your library well. If available, check electronic databases. Learn how to locate a variety of materials that will give you a thorough (not one-sided) view of your topic. (See "Using the computer for research.") When you do find information, take careful notes that include bibliographical information about your source.

Practices for footnoting and preparing a bibliography vary. Therefore, when you're assigned a research paper, ask your instructor to recommend a style guide. Several general guides are available, as well as more specific ones designed for particular fields, among them language and literature, biology, business, history, and law.

Essays arguing a position from a single text

If your assignment is to write about a single text—for example, to take a position on an article in favor of regulating the Internet—read the text more than once. Look up terms you're uncertain about. Mark points that seem unclear or issues that may require research, and include outside research if is allowed by the assignment. (If you do use material from other sources, be sure to cite them, just as you would in a research paper.)

Determine the strongest and weakest arguments in the article. After studying the text carefully, decide whether you agree or disagree with the author's position. Remember that when you write your paper, you should provide a brief, fair summary of that position, whether you're agreeing with it or not. In an argumentative essay you must support your own viewpoint *and* answer the opposition.

Essays analyzing a literary work

When you're asked to analyze a literary work, or one aspect of a literary work, stay close to the text. Read it and, if possible, reread it. Your first job is to interpret meaning, which can take some time. Once you feel comfortable with your interpretation, take notes or mark the text with an eye to finding support for your topic and thesis. You'll be using quotations in your paper, so indicate those passages or lines that might be particularly effective.

Generally, when you write an essay on a nonliterary text, you focus on content, concentrating on the author's information and the quality of his or her arguments. When you write about a literary text, however, you must also pay close attention to the author's technique. If you don't already know such terms as *meter, image, metaphor, simile, diction, flat character,* and *irony,* check a glossary of literary terms. In your notes include specific words and images from the text, observations about structure (a poem's rhyme scheme, for example, or a novel's subplot), point of view, and tone. Remember, however, that when you discuss formal features like these in your essay, you should relate them to a point you are making, usually about the author's theme or purpose. Don't risk having your reader ask, "So *what* if the rhyme scheme changes in the last stanza?"

Narrative, descriptive, and autobiographical essays

For some essays, you'll use your own thoughts, observations, and experiences, without reference to a text. But as with essays of argument and analysis, you need to gather information to develop your main ideas, and taking notes is a good way to do it. Before beginning an essay describing your Aunt Gladys, for example, write down all the details you can about her, including any anecdotes that reveal her characteristics. At this point don't worry about organizing your observations. Remember that you're gathering information. If you haven't yet written a sentence stating a main idea, try to do so now. (For example, *Although Aunt Gladys prides herself on being no trouble to anyone, she finds ways to get everyone in the family to do what she wants,* or *Aunt Gladys looks like a little old lady, but she acts like a teenage girl.)* Without a controlling idea, your essay will be a list of details with nothing to unify them or give them purpose.

When a college application asks for an essay about yourself, your purpose will be to describe the traits, experiences, interests, achievements, and goals that show you're a good candidate for college admission. First, take notes about yourself—whatever you can think of. Be sure to consider things that emphasize your individuality. In going over your notes later, you may decide not to include the no-hit Little League softball game you pitched when you were nine, or every fast-food job you've ever had; but by making a complete list, you can look for patterns that will help you organize your essay. When it comes time to put your points in order, throw out unnecessary details, consolidating and summarizing—for example, mentioning that you held five fast-food jobs (but not specifying each employer) while attending high school and becoming class valedictorian.

Chapter Checkout

Q&A

1. Determine whether the following passages should be quoted or paraphrased.

  a. "It was the best of times; it was the worst of times." (Dickens 1)

  b. "Dr. Kamdibe knew that he was close to his discovery in early February. By the following April, even the media had been alerted to the revolutionary work his lab was conducting. Finally, in June, the cure was announced." (Smith 32).

  c. "Shall I compare thee to a summer's day?" (Shakespeare 18).

2. Suggest a pattern of organization based upon the following essay assignments.

  a. Write about the life of Martin Luther King.

  b. Write about the two presidential candidates.

  c. Explain why auto fatalities are down this year.

  d. Explain why laughter is the best medicine.

3. True or False: The following statements are all true about writing.

  a. You will use all of the material you find when you research.

  b. You do not have to cite new information that you find in a current magazine or Internet site.

  c. When in doubt, it is better to cite your sources.

  d. Paraphrases should be used to summarize long passages in your essays.

  e. Numerous long quotations are necessary in good essays.

  f. Outlines are essential for good essays.

ANSWERS: 1. a. quote b. paraphrase c. quote 2. a. Chronological: birth to death b. Comparison and/or contrast c. Inductive organization leading to a conclusion d. Deductive organization giving specific examples to prove this fact. 3. a. False b. False c. True d. True e. False f. True.

Chapter 15

WRITING

Chapter Check-In

❑ Drafting an interesting and leading introduction

❑ Creating good paragraphs

❑ Developing organized outlines

❑ Writing powerful conclusions

A common misconception about writing is that the first draft must be perfect. However, even excellent writers create multiple drafts before they feel content with their writing. In the first draft, focus on introductions, connecting ideas within paragraphs, and conclusions.

A good introduction catches the reader's attention and then provides a general orientation to the topic. You can interest the reader by using quotations, anecdotes, questions or addressing the reader directly. Paragraphs develop a single idea in a series of connected sentences. A unified paragraph stays focused on a single idea and is coherent and well developed. Your final statement should bring all of your points to their logical conclusion. You can leave the reader pondering your essay by using a quotation, a reference back to a point or question made in the introduction, or a story that emphasizes your thesis.

Working from a Thesis Statement

The first thing to look at when you're ready to organize your paper is your main idea or thesis statement. Putting yourself in a reader's place, imagine how you would expect to see the main idea developed. Then look at the notes you've taken. If you used your thesis statement as a guide in gathering information, you should see a pattern.

Look at the following thesis statement:

> Imposing sanctions on China would be a mistake because it would hurt the American economy, because sanctions are notoriously unsuccessful as a way to force change, and because the United States should not interfere in the internal policies of other countries.

This statement suggests that the paper will be divided into three main parts; it even indicates an order for those sections. When you go through your notes, decide where each note most logically fits. For example, a note about U.S. clothing manufacturers' increasing use of Chinese labor would fit into section one, and a note about the failure of sanctions in the Middle East in section two.

Of course, things aren't usually this neat. Your thesis statement might not be this precise, or the kind of essay you're writing might not lend itself to such an easy division. But starting from the moment you look at your topic and decide on your main idea, you should be thinking about ways to develop it. This thinking leads you to your organizing principle.

A review of some common methods of organization will help you. Remember, however, to avoid an overly rigid approach. After you begin to write, you may realize that your plan needs to be changed. Writing itself, often generates new ideas, or suggests a different direction.

Spatial or chronological organization

Some topics lend themselves to organization based on space or time. A descriptive essay might work well if you begin with a distant view and move closer—first describe how a barn looks from the road, for example, then describe the view you see when you stand directly in front of the barn, then describe the view (and smell and sounds) when standing inside the barn door, and completing your description with what you see when you climb the ladder into the loft.

In the narration of an event and in some kinds of technical writing—describing a process, for example—you write about events in the order they occur. Often dividing your material into stages avoids the "and then, and then, and then!" effect. If you were writing about making a ceramic vase, you could divide the process into three main stages—selecting and preparing the clay, forming and refining the shape of the vase on the potter's wheel, and glazing the piece and firing it in a kiln. The detailed steps in making the vase could then be organized sequentially under these sections.

Dividing a subject into categories

Just as you can divide a process into stages, you can divide a subject into categories. When you look over your notes, and using your thesis statement as a guide, see if logical groupings emerge. Look at the following topic and thesis statement, written by a fictional student.

TOPIC   Write a paper addressing an environmental concern and suggesting ideas for a solution.

THESIS   The United States is losing its forests, and the solution is everyone's responsibility.

Note that the second half of this thesis statement is weak: *the solution is everyone's responsibility* is a vague assertion.

In looking over his notes, the student quickly identifies those that relate to the first part of the thesis statement (*Less than 10 percent of US. old-growth forests remain, U.S. consumption of wood is up 30 percent since 1930, and so on*). However, when he looks at the rest of his notes, he finds he has everything from *Logging bans have been effective in many areas* to *Don't use disposable diapers*, to *Agricultural waste can be effectively processed to make building materials that provide excellent insulation.*

At this point he decides to create categories. He finds that many notes are related to simple, everyday actions that can help reduce wood and paper consumption *(no disposable diapers, e-mail instead of memos, cloth bags instead of paper bags, recycling newspapers, etc.).* Still others cover alternatives for wood, such as *agricultural waste, engineered wood manufactured by the forest-products industry, the use of steel studs in construction rather than wooden ones, a method of wall forming called "rammed earth construction,"* and so on. Then he notices that several notes relate to government actions—*logging bans, wilderness designations, Forest Service reforms*, etc. He decides to use three general classifications as a principle of organization:

    I. Problem

    II. Solutions

       A. Consumer actions

       B. Alternatives to wood

       C. Government regulations

He may decide to change the order of the classifications when he writes his paper, but for now he has a principle of organization.

If some notes don't fit into these classifications, he may want to add another category, or add some subsections. For example, if several notes deal with actions by major conservation groups, he may want to add a division under *Solutions* called *Conservation group activities.* Or, if he finds some notes relating to disadvantages of wood alternatives, he may add some subtopics under B, for example, *price, stability, public perception.*

Dividing material into categories is one of the most basic forms of organization. Make sure the categories are appropriate to the purpose of your paper and that you have sufficient information under each one.

Organizing essays of comparison

Sometimes students have problems with topics that ask them to compare and contrast two things. After gathering information on each thing, they fail to focus on the similarities and dissimilarities between them.

When your topic involves comparison, you can organize in either of two ways. First, you can discuss each thing separately and then include a section in which you draw comparisons and contrasts between them. With this organization, if you were comparing and contrasting two poems, you would write first about one—covering, for example, theme, language, images, tone, and rhyme scheme—and then about the other, covering the same areas. In a third section you would make a series of statements comparing and contrasting major aspects of the poems. If you choose this method, make your separate discussions of the poems parallel—that is, for the second poem, address points in the same order you used for the first poem. Also, in the third section of the paper, avoid simply repeating what you said in sections one and two.

A second way of organizing requires you to decide first which aspects of the poems you want to compare and contrast (theme, language, and imagery) and then to structure your essay according to these. For example, if you begin with theme, you state the themes of both poems and compare them. Then you compare the language of the two poems, then the imagery, then the tone, and so on. Two advantages of this type of organization are, first, you are forced to focus on similarities and dissimilarities and less likely to include material that isn't pertinent and, second, you avoid repetition by eliminating a separate compare-and-contrast section.

You can also combine these two types of organization. For example, you may want to discuss each poem's theme separately, and then move into a point-by-point comparison of the other aspects of the poem (language, imagery, tone, and so on).

Inductive or deductive patterns of organization

In a logical argument, the pattern in which you present evidence and then draw a general conclusion is called *inductive*. This term can also be used to describe a method of approaching your material, particularly in an essay presenting an argument. You are using this method in an essay even when you state the general conclusion *first* and present the supporting evidence in successive paragraphs. In fact, in essays it is customary to begin with the general conclusion as a thesis statement:

EVIDENCE   The student action committee failed to achieve a quorum in all six of its last meetings.

During the past year, the student action committee has proposed four plans for changing the grievance procedure and has been unable to adopt any of them.

According to last month's poll in the student newspaper, 85 percent of the respondents had not heard of the student action committee.

Two openings on the committee have remained unfilled for eight months because no one has applied for membership.

CONCLUSION   The student action committee is an ineffective voice for students at this university.

(Note: In an essay, this would be a thesis statement.)

Another type of organization borrowed from logical argument is called *deductive*. With this pattern you begin with a generalization and then apply it to specific instances. In a timed writing, you might be given a statement such as *It's better to be safe than sorry* or *Beauty is in the eye of the beholder* and then asked to agree or disagree, providing examples that support your view. With such essays, you aren't proving or disproving the truth of a statement, but offering an opinion and then supporting it with examples. For example, if you begin with a generalization such as *Beauty is in the eye of the beholder,* you could cite instances such as different standards for human beauty in different cultures, or different views of beauty in architecture from era to era. You could also use examples from your own experience, such as your brother's appreciation of desert landscapes contrasted to your boredom with them.

Order of examples and evidence

Within any overall pattern of organization, you must decide on the specific order of your examples and evidence. The best plan is to save your most important point or most convincing piece of evidence for last. The last position is the most emphatic, and a reader will expect you to build to your strongest point. Saving the best for last isn't a rule; you must decide, based on your thesis and the evidence and examples you've collected, which order works best. But do remember that you want to avoid having your essay trail off with a trivial example or weak argument.

Connecting paragraphs in an essay

Your essay should move from paragraph to paragraph smoothly, each point growing out of the preceding one. If you are shifting direction or moving to a different point, prepare your reader with a transition. Achieving continuity in your essay is similar to achieving continuity in a paragraph.

Outlining

Creating an **outline**, either a formal or an informal one, helps you stay with your organizational plan. Sometimes an outline helps you see problems in your original plan, and you can eliminate them before you've spent time writing.

If you prefer writing papers without an outline, try an experiment. Create an outline *after* a paper is finished to see if your organization is clear and logical. This exercise may make you decide that outlining is a good idea.

Informal outlines

An *informal outline* can be little more than a list of your main points. You can refine it by following each main point with notations of the evidence or examples that support it. You are, in effect, grouping your notes. A simple outline like this is often all you need. It is especially valuable for timed writings or essay exams. Thinking your approach through before you begin—and jotting your thoughts down—will help you avoid rambling and moving away from the assignment.

Formal outlines

You may want to prepare a more *formal outline*. Sometimes you may even be asked to submit an outline with a writing assignment. Following are a few guidelines:

Use roman numerals for main topics. Alternate letters and Arabic numerals for subtopics. Indent subtopics.

> I.
>> A.
>> B.
>>> 1.
>>> 2.
>>>> a.
>>>> b.

Make outline topics parallel in form. Make subtopics parallel in form also. For example, if you use a sentence for the first topic, use sentences for all subsequent topics, but if you use a noun for the first subtopic, use a noun for the following ones.

Watch the logic of your outline. The main topics generally indicate the basic structure of your essay. The second level of your outline (A, B, C) covers the major ideas that contribute to the larger units. The next level of subtopics is for narrower points related to these ideas. Don't stick irrelevant ideas in your outline under the guise of subtopics. Make sure each element logically fits under its heading or you're defeating the purpose of an outline.

Each topic and subtopic should have at least one mating topic or subtopic, that is, no I without a II, no A without a B, and so on. Remember that topics and subtopics are divisions of your subject, and you can't divide something into one part. If your outline shows solitary topics or subtopics, reevaluate to see whether you are misplacing or poorly stating your headings. The information should perhaps be worked into an existing larger category or divided into two topics or subtopics.

Sentence outlines and topic outlines

In a *sentence outline*, all elements are stated in complete sentences. In a *topic outline*, the elements may be presented as single words or as phrases. Study the following examples.

Sentence outline

> I. Many high school classes do not prepare students for large university classes.
>> A. Nontracked high school classes don't challenge more able students to achieve at the highest level.
>>> 1. Less competition leads some students to "get by" rather than excel.
>>> 2. Inflated grading of good students in nontracked classes can lead to false expectations.

B. High school classes are not designed to encourage individual responsibility, which is required in large university classes.

  1. Required attendance in high school may lead students to react to less rigid attendance requirements by cutting classes.

  2. High school teachers assign daily homework and reading assignments, whereas university professors generally make long-term assignments.

  3. High school teachers frequently spend more time with individual students than do professors in large universities.

II. Some high schools offer programs to help students prepare for university classes.

Topic outline

I. Lack of preparation of high school students for university classes
  A. Nontracked high school classes
    1. Less competition
    2. Mated grades
  B. Less individual responsibility in high school classes
    1. Required attendance
    2. Homework and daily assignments
    3. Individual attention from teachers
II. Programs to prepare high school students for university classes

Getting Started

The first thing to remember when beginning to write is that you don't have to create a perfect first draft. Count on rewriting. Your first draft may well be a mixture of planning and improvising—letting yourself move in a direction you hadn't originally intended. Remember that writing is not a straightforward process, that even when you begin a first draft you may make changes in your thesis statement or in your organizational plan.

The exception to the rule about first drafts is in timed writing assignments, for which you may have time for only one draft. Spend a few moments planning your answer, noting examples you intend to use, and then move ahead. Graders of these assignments are looking for substance, support for your points, clarity, and overall correctness; they will not penalize you for small mechanical errors or for less-than-perfect organization.

Introductions

The opening paragraph of argumentative or analytical papers should both indicate your purpose and establish your tone. The paragraph does not need to be a certain length, though it should be well developed. (For timed writings, an introductory statement rather than a paragraph is sufficient.) An introduction should draw your readers into the paper and make them confident about what you have to say. If you are discussing a particular book, article, or work of art, include its title and author in your opening paragraph.

If you have trouble with introductions, consider coming back to write yours after you have written the rest of your paper. Because an introduction sets the tone as well as introduces the topic, it is better to wait than to churn out a few stale, mechanical sentences.

What to avoid in introductions

Introductions, like all beginnings, are important for setting the tone of your essay. There is no one right way to begin a paper, but there are some things you should keep in mind.

- Avoid obvious general statements or platitudes.

    Drug use is an important issue in high schools today.

    Capital punishment is a very controversial subject.

- Avoid weak or thinly veiled restatements of the assignment.

    It is illuminating to trace the clothing imagery in *King Lear.*

    A person can make many interesting points in comparing the poems "*The Happy Meercat*" and "*Ode to a Wolf.*"

- Avoid flat statements of the thesis or main idea, particularly using *I* or *in this essay.*

    In this paper I will show that the emphasis on winning an Olympic medal is dangerous for young athletes.

    This essay will cover the many opportunities available to young people who choose computer science as a major.

- Avoid definition of a term that doesn't require defining or that leads nowhere.

> The novel *Silas Marner* by George Eliot is about a man who is a miser. What is a miser? According to the definition in *Webster's New World Dictionary*, a miser is "a greedy, stingy person who hoards money for its own sake."

None of these openings make a reader want to continue reading.

Suggestions for introductions

An **introduction** should lead naturally into the rest of your paper and be appropriate to its subject and tone. Some suggestions for openings follow, but use judgment in applying them. Although beginning with an anecdote can be effective for some papers, don't force one where it doesn't belong. A story about your indecisive father is not the best way to begin a paper analyzing the character of *Hamlet*.

Use a relevant quotation from the work you are discussing.

> "I am encompassed by a wall, high and hard and stone, with only my brainy nails to tear it down. And I cannot do it." Kerewin Holmes, one of the main characters in Keri Hulme's novel *The Bone People,* describes herself as both physically and emotionally alone in a tower she has built by the New Zealand Sea. Throughout the novel Hulme uses concrete images—the tower, muteness, physical beatings, the ocean—to suggest her characters' isolation from each other and the community around them.

Provide background or context for your thesis statement.

> Until the second half of this century, Americans spent the country's natural resources freely. They mined for minerals, diverted rivers, replaced wilderness with cities and towns. In the process they cut down forests that had been in place for thousands of years. Now, as the twenty-first century approaches, the reality that progress has its price is obvious to almost everyone. Only ten percent of old-growth forests in the United States remain intact, with demand for wood products expected to grow by fifty percent in the next fifty years. The country is in danger of losing its forests altogether unless citizens pursue solutions from everyday recycling to using wood alternatives to actively supporting government regulations.

Ask a question that leads to your thesis statement.

> *Is the United States still a country where the middle class thrives?* Strong evidence suggests that the traditional American view of a successful middle class is fading. At the very least, the prospects for someone who stands in the economic middle have significantly changed since the 1970s. Twenty-five years ago middle-class people expected to own their own homes in the suburbs and send their children to college. Today, for many people, these expectations have become more like distant dreams. Two factors—a growing disparity in wages within the labor force and rising prices for real estate and goods—suggest that the middle class is a less comfortable place to be than it was for the previous generation.

Begin with a relevant anecdote that leads to your thesis statement.

> Doug was the star in my high school senior class. He captained the football team, dated the best looking girls, charmed the teachers, and managed to get A's and B's seemingly without studying. When he headed off to a big Midwestern university, we weren't surprised. But when he was home again a year later on academic probation, many of us wondered what could have happened. Doug told me candidly that his year at the university was far removed from anything he'd experienced in high school. Quite simply, his small, noncompetitive high school classes hadn't prepared him for a large, impersonal university where the professors didn't know his name, let alone his role as a big man on campus. I believe programs to help students like Doug make the transition from high school to college could help reduce the high failure rate among college freshmen.

Speak directly to your readers. Ask them to imagine themselves in a situation you create.

> Imagine being escorted into a room and asked to disrobe every time you want to take an airplane trip. Picture someone in a uniform grilling you about your background or even hooking you up to a lie detector. Such scenarios seem impossible in America, but experts agree that the United States may be forced to take extreme measures to combat increasing domestic terrorism.

Your own particular topic may suggest to you any number of creative beginnings. Try to go beyond the obvious. For example, which of the following two openings for an essay on the qualities of a good mate is more likely to catch a reader's interest?

> STUDENT 1   It is important to look for many qualities in the person you choose to spend your life with.

STUDENT 2   Finding a mate is hard enough. Finding a mate you're happy with may seem close to impossible.

The Paragraph

A **paragraph** develops one idea with a series of logically connected sentences. Most paragraphs function as small essays themselves, each with a main topic (stated or implied) and several related sentences that support it.

How many paragraphs do you need in your paper? That depends on what you have to say. The idea that an essay should consist of five paragraphs—an introduction, three paragraphs of examples, and a conclusion—is much too rigid, though students first learning to write are sometimes taught this. You may well have more than three examples or points to make, and you may have an example or point that requires several paragraphs of development in itself. Don't limit yourself. Let your particular topic and supporting points guide you in creating your paragraphs.

Paragraph length

Paragraphs vary in length. For example, short paragraphs (one to three sentences) are used in newspaper stories where the emphasis is on reporting information without discussion, or in technical writing where the emphasis is on presenting facts such as statistics and measurements without analysis. Written dialogue also consists of short paragraphs, with a new paragraph for each change of speaker. In an essay, a short paragraph can also be effectively used for dramatic effect or transition.

> But the reconciliation was never to take place. Her grandmother died as Jane was driving home from the airport.

Generally, however, avoid a series of very short paragraphs in your essays. They suggest poor development of an idea.

On the other hand, paragraphs a page or more in length are difficult for most readers, who like to see a subject divided into shorter segments. Look carefully at long paragraphs to see whether you have gone beyond covering one idea or are guilty of repetition, wordiness, or rambling. Don't arbitrarily split a long paragraph in half by indenting a particular sentence, however. Make sure that each paragraph meets the requirement of a single main idea with sentences that support it.

Paragraph unity

A **unified paragraph** is one that focuses on one idea and one idea only. Look at the following example of a paragraph that *lacks* unity.

Identification of particular genes can lead to better medicine. For example, recently scientists identified a defective gene that appears to cause hemochromatosis, or iron overload. Iron overload is fairly easily cured if it is recognized and treated early, but currently it is often misdiagnosed because it mimics more familiar conditions. The problem is that when not treated in time, iron overload leads to a variety of diseases, from diabetes to liver cancer. The identification of the faulty gene can prevent misdiagnosis by allowing physicians, through a screening test, to identify patients who carry it and treat them before the condition becomes too advanced. *It is interesting that most people don't realize the exact role of iron in the body.* They know that it is important for their health, but few are aware that only about ten percent of the iron in food is normally absorbed by the small intestine. Most of the rest is tied up in hemoglobin, which carries oxygen from the lungs.

The first sentence of the paragraph presents the main idea that identification of genes leads to improved medical care. This idea is developed by the example of how the identification of a gene causing iron overload can lead to better diagnosis and early treatment. In the italicized sentence the paragraph begins to wander. It is a topic sentence for a different paragraph, one about the role of iron in the body and not about a benefit of genetic research.

Sometimes a sentence or two buried in the middle of a paragraph can break its unity, as in the following example.

Moving out of my parents' house and into an apartment didn't bring me the uncomplicated joy that I had expected. First of all, I had to struggle to make the rent every month, and the landlord was much less understanding than my parents. Then I realized I had to do my own laundry, clean up the place now and then, and fix my own meals. *One nice thing about my mother is that she is an excellent cook. She even attended a French cooking school before she married my father.* It's true that I liked the greater freedom I had in my apartment—no one constantly asking me what time I'd be home, no one nagging me about cleaning up my room or raking the front lawn—but I wasn't thrilled with spending most of a Saturday getting rid of a cockroach infestation, or Sunday night doing three loads of smelly laundry.

Notice how the italicized sentences interrupt the flow of the paragraph, which is really about the down side of leaving home and not about the writer's mother.

To test the unity of your paragraphs, locate your topic sentence (if you have left it unstated, be clear on your paragraph's main idea) and then test the other sentences to see if they are developing that particular idea or if they are wandering off in another direction.

Paragraph coherence

Along with developing a single idea, a paragraph should be well organized. You can use many of the same principles—chronology, inductive and deductive patterns, and so on—that you use to organize complete essays.

Once you've decided on the order of your details, make sure the connections between sentences in the paragraph are clear. The smooth, logical flow of a paragraph is called **paragraph coherence.** Write each sentence with the previous one in mind.

Connecting sentences through ideas

Connect your sentences through their content, by picking up something from one and carrying it into the next.

Follow a sentence that makes a general point with a specific, clear illustration of that point. Look at the following example.

> The gap in pay between people with basic skills and people without them seems to be widening. In one comparison, the pay difference between women of varied mathematical skills had grown from $.93 an hour in 1978 to $1.71 an hour in 1986.

Here, the second sentence is a clear illustration of the point made in the first sentence. But look at how coherence can be lost in a paragraph.

> The gap in pay between people with basic skills and people without them seems to be widening. Women are now playing a more important role in the work force than they have since World War II, when many had to fill the positions of men who were overseas. The pay difference between women of varied mathematical skills has grown considerably, from $.93 an hour in 1978 to $1.71 an hour in 1986.

In this example, the second sentence is not clearly connected to the first. Sentence three returns to the subject, but the continuity of the idea has been weakened.

You can also use one sentence to reflect or comment on the previous sentence, as in the following example.

> The idea that in America hard work leads to financial success has been one of our most successful exports. For decades immigrants

have arrived on American soil with a dream that here they can have what was impossible in their home countries, where they were limited by class structure or few opportunities.

Be sure in reviewing your paragraph that such reflections logically follow from the previous statement. Here, immigrants arriving with the preconceived notion that they will succeed, is tied to the point in the first sentence that the American dream has been a successful export.

You can also connect sentences by asking a question and following it with an answer or making a statement and following it with a question.

> Why should the government invest in research? Research leads to technological advances that create employment, as was shown in the years following World War II.

> Polls indicate that many Americans favor regulation of the Internet. Are they willing to pay both with their tax dollars and their freedoms?

The sentences in these two examples are linked by words as well as by ideas. In the first example, the word *research* has been picked up from the question and repeated in the answer. In the second example, the pronoun *they* in the question has its antecedent *(Americans)* in the previous statement.

Connecting with words and phrases

Achieving paragraph coherence by connecting ideas is your first step. But as indicated in the last two examples, words and phrases can help strengthen the connection between sentences.

■ Use a pronoun whose antecedent appears in the previous sentence.

> *Gabriel Garcia Marquez* suspends the laws of reality in his novels. *He* creates bizarre and even magical situations that reveal character in surprising ways.

■ Repeat a key word or phrase.

> The idea of a perfect society, though never realized, continues to intrigue political *philosophers*. None of *these philosophers* seem to agree on where perfection lies.

■ Use a synonym.

> According to my research, *physical beauty is* still considered a more important asset for women than for men. *Looks* are everything, according to several girls I spoke to, while the boys I interviewed felt that their athletic prowess and social status were at least as important as their appearance.

■ Use word patterns, such as *first, second, third,* and so on.

> The reasons for the dean's announcing his decision today are clear. *First,* students will recognize that he is listening to their concerns. *Second,* faculty will applaud the end of a disruptive period of indecision. *Third,* wealthy and influential alumni—though not particularly pleased by all the details of the plan—will be overjoyed that the controversy will be off the front page of the paper.

■ Use transitional words and phrases. Many words and phrases signal connections between sentences in a paragraph or between paragraphs in a paper. Look at the italicized words in the following sentences.

> The main character worships her. *Later,* his adoration turns to hatred.

> The church stood at the top of the hill. *Below* stretched miles of orchards.

> She treated him well. *For example,* she bought him a car and new clothes.

> The product promised he'd grow new hair. *But* all he grew was a rash.

> Hamlet disdained Ophelia. *As a result,* she killed herself.

> Elizabeth was angry at Darcy. *In fact,* she wanted nothing to do with him.

> The plan is too expensive. *Furthermore, it* won't work.

> No one volunteered to help. *In other words,* no one cared.

In the preceding examples, the italicized words or phrases explicitly connect the second sentence to the first by creating a particular relationship. Vary the transitional words you use.

Following is a list of words classified according to the relationships they suggest.

> **Time or place:** *above, across from, adjacent to, afterward, before, behind, below, beyond, earlier, elsewhere, farther on, here, in the distance, near by, next to, opposite to, to the left, to the right*
>
> **Example:** *for example, for instance, specifically, to be specific*
>
> **Contrast:** *but, however, nevertheless, on the contrary, on the other hand*
>
> **Similarity:** *similarly, in the same way, equally important*

Consequence: *accordingly, as a result, consequently, therefore*

Emphasis: *indeed, in fact, of course*

Amplification: *and, again, also, further, furthermore, in addition, moreover, too*

Restatement: *in other words, more simply stated, that is, to clarify*

Summary and conclusion: *altogether, finally, in conclusion, in short, to summarize*

Conclusions

How should you end your paper? Writing a proper **conclusion** is like tying a ribbon around a gift package. It's the last thing you do, but it also gives your final effort a finishing touch. If your ending works, your reader will feel satisfied.

What to avoid

Before you can write your conclusion you should know what to avoid. Here are some common errors.

■ Don't introduce a new topic. For example, if your essay has been about the loss of forests and possible solutions for the high consumption of wood products, don't end with a paragraph about another environmental concern, such as the disappearance of the California condor.

■ Don't trail off with a weak statement or a statement leaving your reader up in the air.

> The Internet, free of regulation, has opened a world of information and ideas to everyone. Children enjoy learning at the computer.

■ Don't simply repeat your thesis or main idea in the same words.

> Thus, as stated earlier, clothing imagery shows the changes in King Lear throughout the play.

■ Don't apologize for or suggest doubts about your thesis.

> For a variety of reasons, middle-class expectations in the 1990s differ from those in the 1970s. It is possible, however, that the difference is not particularly illuminating about life in the United States.

You may use a brief concluding sentence instead of a formal conclusion in a simple or short paper (up to five pages, for example). Formal conclusions can sometimes be superfluous and even insulting to the reader's intelligence, particularly if the conclusion is a long summary of what he or she just read. Instead, end your paper with your best point, using a strong final sentence.

Suggestions for conclusions

The two most important things a conclusion should do is give your readers a sense of completion and leave them with a strong impression. You can do this with a single statement or with a paragraph. If you do write a concluding paragraph, consider these possibilities.

End with an appropriate quotation:

> Throughout the novel the characters suffer both from their isolation and from their attempts to end it. Kerewin burns her tower, Joe beats his son and goes to prison, and Simon—who barely survives the beating—must painfully find his way back to those he loves. Recurring images dramatize their journeys, which end in a reconciliation between being alone and being part of a community. Kerewin describes the home that will now take the place of her lonely tower: "I decided on a shell-shape, a regular spiral of rooms expanding around the decapitated Tower . . . privacy, apartness, but all connected and all part of the whole."

Notice that in this example the writer also pulls loose ends together and briefly refers to the thesis.

Without directly repeating your thesis, come full circle by relating the final paragraph to a point you made in your introduction.

> Preserving old-growth forests and finding substitutes for wood should concern everyone who cares about the environment. The days when Americans could view this country as an unlimited provider of resources are as gone as roaming herds of buffalo and pioneers in covered wagons.

End with a story related to your thesis.

> On a recent trip to the airport, I stood at the ticket counter behind an angry woman. It seems she'd forgotten her photo ID and was being told by the attendant that she couldn't fly without it. After calling the clerk a storm trooper and threatening to sue the airline, she turned to me indignantly. "You tell me. Do I *look* like the kind of person who would blow up a plane?" I didn't answer, since the

question seemed rhetorical. I wondered, though, how in the future this woman would react to a fifteen-minute interview about herself, or to a uniformed attendant patting her down.

Another way to conclude a paper is to summarize your points. But because summaries aren't particularly interesting conclusions, consider one only if your paper is fairly long and if one would be helpful to your reader. Keep summaries brief and avoid wishy-washy final sentences, such as *For all these reasons, the Internet should not be regulated.*

Chapter Checkout

Q&A

1. Evaluate the following introductions as (E) effective or (I) ineffective.
    a. "You live by the sword; you die by the sword."
    b. In this essay I will prove smoking is dangerous.
    c. Who are the homeless in America?
    d. Homelessness is a big problem.

2. Evaluate the following concluding sentences as (E) effective or (I) ineffective.
    a. Although not all of my conclusions are supportable, I still think this law is dangerous.
    b. As stated above, global warming is a serious concern.
    c. For all these reasons, my position is correct.

3. True or False: All of the following statements about paragraphs are true.
    a. Paragraphs should be divided based on the ideas which they contain.
    b. Paragraphs should always be five sentences long.
    c. Paragraphs have unity if they are focused on a single idea.
    d. A single word or phrase can be a unifying focus for an entire paragraph.

Answers: 1. a. E b. I c. E d. I. 2 a. I b. I c. I. 3. a. True b. False c. True d. True.

Chapter 16
REVISING AND EDITING

Chapter Check-In

❑   Creating essay titles

❑   Reviewing your first draft

❑   Editing to correct grammar and mechanics

❑   Using a revision checklist to prepare a final draft

Since titles are important, choose one that is interesting and informative. Consider the formality of the writing assignment and the audience when selecting a title for your work. Try reading your draft aloud, and if possible, ask someone you trust to review your essay.

After the review is completed, edit and revise the essay. Editing, which can be done with most computers and word processors, involves looking at the grammatical and mechanical content of your work. Revising means looking not only at grammar, but also the overall effect of the essay. Editing and revising ensure that the final draft is appropriate for the assignment and audience, grammatically and mechanically correct, well organized and supported, and well crafted.

Titles

While you're writing an essay, if you have a good idea for a title, write it down. But often the best time to choose a title is when you've completed a first draft and read it over. You'll have a more complete picture of your essay. Be creative, but don't overdo it. For example, if you're writing a paper about deforestation, *"Knock on Wood"* might seem clever, but it doesn't accurately fit the topic.

Use good judgment when you choose a title. Consider the tone of your essay and your audience. *"No More Mr. Nice Guy"* might be a good title for a personal essay on the loss of your gullibility, but think twice before using it as the title of your analytical paper on Shakespeare's character *Macbeth*. (It's true, however, that one instructor who had received dozens of papers with unimaginative titles reacted well to the student who called hers "*Dial 'M' for Murder: The Character of Macbeth.*")

The best advice is to take a middle road. Avoid both dullness and strained cleverness. Consider a good quotation from a work you are writing about, an effective phrase from your own essay, or an appropriate figure of speech:

	"Sleep No More": The Role of Macbeth's Conscience
RATHER THAN	Macbeth's Conscience
	"I'm Nobody" Finding Emily Dickinson in her Poetry
RATHER THAN	Emily Dickinson and her Poetry
	Gaining Safety or Losing Freedom: The Debate over Airport Security Measures
RATHER THAN	Airport Security Measures
	Only Skin Deep?
RATHER THAN	The Importance of Beauty to Today's Woman
	Fit to be Tried: An Examination of the McNaughton Rule
RATHER THAN	Judging Legal Sanity

Reviewing the First Draft

When you read your first draft, you will probably make your most extensive revisions. Here are a few suggestions that can help you in reviewing your first draft.

- If possible, leave some time between writing the first draft and reviewing it. Your objectivity will improve.

- Try reading your paper aloud to yourself; sometimes your ear catches problems your eye misses.

- Ask someone to read your draft and offer suggestions. Choose a reader you can trust to be honest and fair. And remember: You are looking for an objective opinion, not simply reassurance. Judge your reader's suggestions carefully, and decide for yourself their value, and whether or not to act on them.

- Remember that nothing is unchangeable. Until preparation of your final draft, you can change your thesis, your organization, your emphasis, your tone, and so on. A review of your first draft should *not* be limited to minor mechanical errors.

- Use a revision checklist to make sure you've reviewed your draft thoroughly.

Preparing the Final Draft

You may be able to move directly from your revised first draft to a final draft, but careful writers often prepare several drafts before they are ready to call a piece finished. Within your time constraints, follow their example. As you rewrite, you may continue to discover wordy constructions, poor connections, awkward sentences, and so on. Only when you're satisfied that you've done your best should you prepare the final draft.

Writing and editing a draft

The computer allows you to produce a legible first draft that's easy to change by using a few basic functions, such as *delete, insert, merge, block,* and *move.* When you try making changes to a handwritten draft, on the other hand, you can end up with something so messy it's indecipherable. If you want to change a word-processed draft but aren't certain whether you'll want to keep the changes, save both your original and your revised drafts under different file names and decide later which you want to use— or import parts of one into the other. You can also re-order the paragraphs in a paper with a few keystrokes.

You can do much of your editing directly on the screen. If you think of a better way to say what you've just said, make the change immediately and move on. For more global editing, however, many writers like to print out sections or complete drafts, mark them up by hand, and then go back to the computer to input the changes. This method has advantages. Working on the screen limits you to a small section of text; scrolling back and forth in the document can be confusing, and it's difficult to get a beginning-to-end picture of what you've written. Another advantage of printing out your document is that it forces you to slow down and read carefully. Sometimes, because you can write so quickly on a computer, your fingers may get ahead of your thoughts. Remember that good writing requires deliberation and judgment, and that you should always review a computer draft closely.

Spell-checking, grammar-checking, and search-and-replace functions

A spell-check function is useful for catching misspelled words, typos, and accidental repetitions *(the the)*. But be careful. The checker won't signal a word that is actually a word, even if it isn't the one you intended—for example, when you inadvertently type *form* for *from*. Spell-checking also doesn't distinguish between homonyms, so if you have trouble with *its* and *it's,* it won't help you. Consider the spell-checker as an aid, not a replacement for your own careful proofreading.

Grammar or style-checkers require even more caution because grammar and style are less clear-cut than spelling. Many writers don't use these functions at all, and unless you already have a good grasp of grammar, they can be confusing or misleading. For example, the checkers will catch pronoun agreement and reference errors but not dangling participles or faulty parallelism. Some checkers flag possible homonym confusions, usage problems (literal used incorrectly, for example), and passive constructions, but they also signal every sentence beginning with But, all contractions, and every sentence ending with a preposition—"errors" that current usage generally permits. If you use a checking function, do so critically. Don't automatically change a passive construction, or restructure a sentence ending with a preposition, for example, simply because the checker flags it.

A *search-and-replace* feature in word-processing programs lets you correct a particular error throughout your paper automatically. If you find you've misspelled a person's name, you can spell it correctly and ask the program to locate every instance of the name in your 25-page document and replace it with the correct version. Just be sure that the error is one that you want replaced in the same way every time.

Layout of the final draft

With word processing, you can produce a final draft that looks professional. Choose from different type fonts, use boldface type and italics, center titles with a stroke, create headings of different sizes, and use bullets or other symbols to highlight your points. You can create properly formatted and numbered footnotes, and place them correctly by selecting a footnote option and consistent page numbers by selecting automatic page numbering. If it's appropriate, you might want to present some materials in tables, charts, or graphs—which are easy to create with most programs. You can even import graphics. One note of warning: Don't confuse a good-looking paper with a well-written one. Although your readers may be favorably disposed towards documents that are nice to look at, word-processing features can't compensate for meager content or poorly expressed ideas.

Checklist

Good writing often comes after revision and rewriting. If you can view your work critically, you will be able to improve it. Use the following checklist before you write a final draft.

Purpose, audience, and tone

These three elements deal with the overall effect of your essay and should guide you throughout your writing.

- If I am writing in response to an assignment, does my essay fulfill all parts of the assignment?

- Is my topic too broad?

- Do I state my thesis or main idea early in the paper? If I don't state a thesis or main idea, is it clearly implied so that there can be no mistake about my purpose?

- Is my thesis or main idea interesting? If this is an essay of argument, is my thesis statement fair? Do I take opposing viewpoints into account?

- Have I thought about my audience? Does my audience have any special requirements? Is my tone appropriate to my audience and purpose?

- Is my tone consistent throughout the essay?

Examples, evidence, and details

These are specific details in the writing process. When you read your essay, you can determine whether you have used these elements well.

- Have I adequately developed my thesis or main idea? Do I use specific details rather than generalities?

- Are my examples and evidence accurate, relevant, and convincing?

- Do I use quotations appropriately? Is too much of my paper quotation? Do I paraphrase carefully?

- Do I cite sources for the words and ideas of others?

Structure

Use an outline to determine the structure of your paper, but be aware that you may need to alter it as you write. Keep in mind the following:

- Do I have a principle of organization? Do I avoid repetition and digressions?

- Is my organization appropriate to my topic and thesis?

- Do I adequately introduce and conclude my paper?

- Are my paragraphs well developed, unified, and coherent?

- Does one paragraph grow out of another? Do I use transitions?

- Are my examples, evidence, and details in the best order? Do I save the strongest point for last?

Language and style

Rely on a dictionary and your word-processing tools to help you with language and style. Ask yourself some questions.

- Have I chosen my words carefully? Am I sure of meanings?

- Is my language appropriate to my purpose, tone, and audience?

- Have I avoided wordy expressions? euphemisms? clichés?

- Have I avoided pretentious language?

- Have I used idioms correctly?

- Have I followed the guidelines of current written usage?

- Have I avoided sexism in the use of nouns and pronouns?

- Have I preferred the active to the passive voice of the verb?

Sentence construction

Use your editing and revision skills to make sure your sentences are well constructed. Keep the following in mind:

- Are my sentences correct? Have I avoided both fragments and run-ons?

- Are my modifiers in the right place? Do I have any dangling modifiers?

- Do my subjects and predicates agree in number?

- Do I keep parallel constructions parallel?

- Have I avoided short, choppy sentences?

- Do I combine sentences effectively?

- Are my sentences varied in length and structure? Do I avoid monotony?

Grammar

Use this book to augment your grammar skills and keep in mind the following:

- Have I checked

    spelling (including correct plural forms, hyphenation)

    capitalization

    correct use and consistency of verb tenses

    agreement (nouns, verbs, pronouns)

    pronoun cases

    pronoun antecedents

    use of adjectives with linking verbs

    comparative degrees of adjectives and adverbs

- Does my punctuation make my meaning clear? Have I followed punctuation rules?

- Commas with nonrestrictive elements; no commas with restrictive elements

- Commas with interrupting elements, with introductory phrases and clauses when necessary, between series items, between independent clauses

- Correct use of periods and question marks

- Correct use (and not overuse) of exclamation points

- Correct use of semicolons and colons

- Correct use (and not overuse) of dashes and parentheses

- Correct use (and not overuse) of quotation marks

- Correct use of other punctuation with quotation marks

Chapter Checkout

Q&A

1. Evaluate the following titles as (E) effective or (I) ineffective.

  a. Capital Punishment
  b. Skiing Vail: Tips for the Best Vacation on the Slopes
  c. The Magical World of Entomology: Bugs
  d. *"The Philadelphia Story"*: Cary Grant's Finest Film

2. Identify whether the following steps in the writing process should be done in the (1) first draft or in the (2) final draft stage.

  a. Writing a conclusion
  b. Creating a title
  c. Writing an introduction
  d. Checking spelling

3. True or False: All of the following are revision considerations.

  a. Am I doing the correct assignment?
  b. Have I considered the audience?
  c. Do I have a minimum of five supporting main ideas?
  d. Do I use transitions between and within paragraphs?
  e. Have I checked spelling and grammar?

Answers: 1. a. I b. E. c. I d. E. 2. a. 1 b. 2 c. 1 d. 2. 3. a. True b. True c. False d. True e. True.

CQR REVIEW

Use this CQR Review to practice what you've learned in this book and to build your confidence in the grammar, usage and style skills necessary for good writing. After you work through the review questions, the problem solving exercises, and the fun and useful practice projects, you will be well on your way to achieving your goal of writing well.

Q&A

Chapter 1-5

1. Identify the part of speech of the underlined word(s) in the following sentences.

   a. Judy and Tony plan to visit <u>Ireland</u> again this year.
   b. Will mother go with <u>them</u> this time?
   c. The daisies are a <u>little</u> wilted, but still pretty.
   d. She went <u>reluctantly</u> to the gym.
   e. <u>To love</u> him is to accept his eccentricities.
   f. Arriving before the others, Edward was very <u>eager</u> to get to work.

Chapter 6-7

2. Identify the common sentence errors in the sentences below. If there are no errors write N in the blank.

   a. Although he had excellent test scores, Stan did not think his application was impressive since he had not participated in any extra curricular activities. _____
   b. I am waiting for the bus it started to rain. _____
   c. The hushed colors and heavier textures of Nicholas Razinski in his later, often called his darker or more mature period. _____
   d. In order to book the trip we had to wait for the agent and have patience. _____

Chapter 8–10

3. Fill in the blank: Add correct punctuation to the following sentences. If punctuation is not needed write N in the blank.

  a. I have labeled all the plants by kingdom and phylum ____ This will aid us in the following ____ research ____ review ____ and ____ presentation of our science project ____

  b. Does she know ____ although it does not really matter ____ about the reward for the lost child ____

  c. "Stop ____ " she exclaimed in terror ____

  d. "This product is flammable ____ " ____ Erik read aloud ____

Chapter 11

4. Multiple Choice: Choose the correct word to complete the sentences below.

  a. The market correction should not effect/affect home sales in the year ahead.

  b. Beside/Besides, I am getting a new computer next month.

  c. It's/Its not quite as cold as the report predicted.

  d. The diversity of it's/its students was a strength of the program.

  e. Lay/Lie your glasses where you can see them.

  f. My cat, Minka, lays/lies at the foot of the bed each night.

  g. She lay/laid the perfume on my desk yesterday.

  h. Yesterday he lay/laid down for a nap on the porch swing.

  i. He spotted there/their/they're mistake immediately.

  j. There/Their/They're are only a few participants in the study.

  k. There/Their/They're the best friends we have in town.

Chapter 12

5. True or False: The following sentences are not wordy.

  a. Being the woman in the front office, Carol was accustomed to frequent intrusions.

  b. We stayed until after the conclusion of the movie to see the credits.

  c. Although the rain never relented, Claire played in the tennis tournament all day.

  d. The fact is that few are aware of the importance of the wetlands.

  e. Because of her new haircut, she felt like a different person.

Chapter 13-14

6. Identify the following as topic (TP) or thesis (TH).

a. The Luddite movement in England had a tremendous impact on labor relations.

b. The popularity of Marxism in Universities despite the fall of Communism in Eastern Europe.

c. The Pre-Raphaelite brotherhood and the art of Dante Gabriel Rossetti.

d. Origami is a beautiful art form that requires simplicity and precision.

Chapter 15-16

7. True or False: All of the following statements about writing are true.

a. Writers should acknowledge by citation or quotation all information they borrow.

b. Introductions should never state the thesis main ideas directly.

c. Conclusions should repeat the information in the introduction.

d. Paragraphs should break when their focus changes.

e. Titles should be a rewording of the thesis sentence.

f. Correcting spelling and grammar are all that are necessary once you have a first draft.

Answers: 1. a. proper noun b. pronoun replacing unknown noun c. adverb modifying the adjective wilted d. adverb modifying the verb went e. abstract noun f. adjective modifying Edward. **2.** a. N b. Run on c. fragment d. faulty parallelism. **3.** a. I have labeled all the plants by kingdom and phylum <u>period or semicolon</u> This will aid us in the following areas <u>colon</u> research <u>comma</u> review <u>comma</u> and <u>N</u> presentation of our science project <u>period</u> b. Does she know <u>comma or dash</u> although it does not really matter <u>comma or dash</u> about the reward for the lost child <u>question mark</u> c. "Stop <u>exclamation point</u> " she exclaimed in terror <u>period</u> d. "This product is flammable <u>comma</u> " <u>N</u> Erik read aloud <u>period.</u> **4.** a. affect b Beside c. It's d. its e. Lay f. lies g. laid h. lay i. their j. There k. They're. **5.** a. False b. False c. True d. False e. True. **6.** a. TH b. TP c. TP d. TH. (See Chapter 14 for additional help with topic and thesis sentences.) **7.** a. True b. False c. False d. True e. False f. False.

Critical Thinking

Chapter 1

1. Collective nouns do what?

2. How do you make subjects and verbs agree?

3. What is the difference between plural and possessive?

Chapter 2

4. What is an infinitive?

5. What is a gerund?

Chapter 3

6. When do you use who and when do you use whom?

Chapter 4–5

7. What is the difference between comparative and superlative adjectives and adverbs?

Chapter 6

8. What is the difference between an independent and a subordinate clause?

Chapter 7

9. How do you correct a run-on sentence?

10. What is a sentence fragment?

Chapter 8

11. When should you use an exclamation point?

Chapter 9

12. When do you use a colon and when do you use a semicolon?

Chapter 10

13. Where does punctuation belong in a quotation?

Chapter 11

14. What are idioms and how do you use them correctly?

Chapter 12

15. How do you spell compound adjectives and adverbs?

Chapter 13-14

16. What should you do before you start writing?

17. Why is an outline important?

18. How do you avoid plagiarism?

Chapter 15–16

19. What should a good introduction do?

20. What does a good conclusion do?

21. What is the purpose of revision and editing?

Real-World Scenarios

1. Write an essay about capital punishment. Discuss the steps that you will take to complete this assignment.

2. How would you outline an essay for a paper about the life of Gandhi? How would this be different from an outline for a paper that argues against gun control?

3. You learn a lot about a new topic from one very good book. How do you decide what to quote, what to paraphrase, and what to cite in your essay?

Answers: 1.To begin, identify the purpose, audience and narrow your topic. For example, one approach to this assignment might be to write an argument to persuade the readers of a newspaper to support capital punishment for a specific crime. Next, you will need a thesis or sentence that makes an assertion about your topic. Then, you will begin researching and organizing your ideas. A good writer would then outline and begin writing using the outline as their guide. Finally, you should revise and edit, creating new drafts of your writing, to correct mistakes and improve the organization and style. 2. The purpose of the essay often dictates the organization and outline format. The essay about Gandhi is an informative essay. The traditional way to organize an informative essay about an individual's life is to move chronologically from birth to death. The gun control argument has a persuasive, not an informative, purpose. As a result, it should not be organized around a chronological history of gun control measures. A better strategy would be to organize the essay around a series of reasons or main ideas that prove your position. The outlines and organization are different because the purpose of the assignments is different. 3. Anytime you are using ideas or words from another writer you must identify this with a quotation or citation. The one exception to this rule is that information considered common knowledge does not need to be identified. What this means is that you should first determine whether the information you want to use in your essay is information that the average person would know. If it is not, then you must use a citation to let the reader know where the information came from even if you are not directly quoting the other author. Quotes should generally be used to provide additional support to your ideas, or when the quotation is so eloquent or powerful that a paraphrase would not provide the same result. Paraphrases are generally used to summarize or explain long passages from another author's work. Deciding when to use each is a stylistic consideration that can vary dramatically with each writer. A good rule to remember is that you never want to use so many quotes that it looks as though the other author is writing your paper.

Practice Projects

1. Talk to people who are good writers and ask them what they think are good writing strategies.

2. Keep copies of everything you write and periodically review your writing to revise, edit, and improve it.

3. Ask a friend to read your writing or visit a writing center to get feedback about your writing.

4. Take a writing class and get involved! Practice will always improve your writing.

CQR RESOURCE CENTER

CQR Resource Center offers the best resources available in print and online to help you study and review the core concepts of grammar, usage and style. You can find additional resources, plus study tips and tools to help test your knowledge, at www.cliffsnotes.com.

Books

This CliffsNotes book is one of many great books about writing. If you are interested in additional resources, then we suggest the following publications:

The Elements of Style, by Strunk, et al., is a popular guide in high schools with students and teachers alike. Allyn & Bacon, $6.95.

The Chicago Manual of Style: The Essential Guide for Writers, Editors and Publishers, (14th Edition), has set the standard since 1909 for editing primarily in periodicals (magazines, journals, newspapers). University of Chicago Press, $45.00.

Publication Manual of the American Psychological Association, (4th Edition), is the essential reference guide for writers in the fields of behavioral and social sciences. American Psychological Association, $21.95.

MLA Handbook for Writers of Research Papers, (5th Edition), will answer any question you might have about writing a research paper on a topic in the humanities. Modern Languages Association, $14.75.

The Gregg Reference Manual, by William A. Sabin, is an indispensable resource for business writers. McGraw Hill Text, $27.28.

How To Say It: Choice Words, Phrases, Sentences, and Paragraphs for Every Situation, by Rosalie Maggio, provides some wonderful models of business and personal letters for any situation. Prentice Hall Press, $15.95.

Bird by Bird: Some Instructions on Writing and Life, by Anne Lamott, provides some useful and witty observations about the writing process and practical exercises to improve your writing. Anchor, $12.95.

The Writer's Idea Book, by Jack Heffron, suggests numerous writing exercises to improve your confidence and your writing style. Writers Digest Books, $18.99.

Sin and Syntax: How to Craft Wickedly Effective Prose, by Constance Hale, focuses on the relationship between grammar and style in writing. Broadway Books, $16.00.

Wiley also has three Web sites that you can visit to read about all the books we publish:

- www.cliffsnotes.com

- www.dummies.com

- www.wiley.com

Internet

W. Strunk Elements of Style, www.bartleby.com/141/index.html, provides online answers to all your style questions based upon the guidelines outlined in their famous handbook.

Harvard University Writing Center, www.fas.harvard.edu/ ~wricntr/wtools.html, provides an on-line book, writing handouts, and links to writing resources.

www.library.com, will connect you with libraries across the country and links to homework helpers in every subject.

Next time you are on the Internet, don't forget to drop by www. cliffsnotes.com. We created an online Resource Center that you can use today, tomorrow, and beyond.

Glossary

action verb a verb that animates a sentence, either physically or mentally.

active voice see *voice.*

additive phrase an expression typically set off with commas, that while it seems to be part of the subject is not, and therefore does not change the number of the verb.

adjective a word that modifies a noun, pronoun.

adverb a word that modifies a noun, pronoun, or another adverb.

adverbial clause subordinate clauses that begin with subordinate conjunctions; they function as adverbs within the sentence and cannot stand alone as sentences.

agreement see *pronoun agreement* or *subject-predicate agreement.*

antecedent the noun or group of words acting as a noun to which the pronoun refers.

appositive a word or group of words that restates or identifies the noun or pronoun it is next to.

audience refers to the reader at the other end of your writing; you should consider your audience's position and experiences when deciding on the appropriate language, style, and tone for your essay.

case refers to the way a noun or pronoun is used in a phrase, clause, or sentence; case can be subjective, objective, or possessive.

clause a group of related words, but unlike a phrase, a clause has a subject and predicate.

cliché trite, overused expressions, many of which rely on figurative language and should be avoided in writing.

collective noun a word that stands for a group of things is called a collective noun.

colon used primarily when introducing a list, introducing a quotation or formal statement, or introducing a restatement or explanation.

comma the most frequently used internal punctuation in sentences; commas are used after introductory clauses and phrases, with restrictive and nonrestrictive elements, with appositives, between items in a series, between modifiers in a series, to join independent clauses, and to set off interrupting elements.

comma splice see *run-on sentence.*

comparative degree used with adjectives and adverbs to compare two people, things, or actions.

complement (predicate nominative or predicate adjective) an element in a predicate that identifies or describes the subject; a complement can be either a noun (called a predicate noun or predicate nominative), or an adjective (called a predicate adjective).

complete predicate the verb or verb phrase and the words that modify or complete it.

complete subject the noun or pronoun and the words that modify or complete it.

complex sentence contains one independent clause and one or more subordinate clauses.

compound adjectives adjectives that are hyphenated when they appear before a noun.

compound adverbs while most compound adverbs are written as two words, those beginning with *over* or *under* are spelled as one word.

compound preposition prepositions made up of more than one word.

compound sentence has two or more independent clauses, joined by coordinating conjunctions, and no subordinate clauses.

compound subjects refers to more than one actor in a sentence.

compound word combination of two words can create a spelling problem; a dictionary is your best guide to correct spelling.

compound-complex sentence joins two or more independent clauses with one or more subordinate clauses.

conclusions the final paragraph or paragraphs of an essay, and should give a reader a sense of completion.

conjunction words that join or link elements.

conjunctive (sentence) adverbs words that look like coordinating conjunctions but are actually adverbs.

coordinating conjunction (*and, but, for, nor, or, so,* and *yet*) join words, phrases, or clauses that are grammatically equal in rank.

correlative conjunction conjunctions that come in matched pairs, like not only/but also.

dangling modifiers are similar to misplaced modifiers except that the modifier is not just separated from the word it modifies; it is missing the word it modifies.

dash a punctuation device used to interrupt a sentence, or introduce a restatement or explanation.

demonstrative pronoun (*this, that, these, those*) single out what you are talking about.

direct object a noun that receives the action of the sentence but that is not the subject.

draft a written version of an essay; most writers create multiple drafts in the process of writing.

ellipsis   indicates an omission from a quotation.

elliptical clause   a clause in which a word or words have been omitted.

euphemism   a mild or roundabout word or phrase used in place of one considered painful or offensive.

exclamation point   follow interjections and other expressions of strong feeling; they may also lend force to a command.

faddish words   terms that appear suddenly and become very popular in language; some last, some fade, and some disappear altogether.

faulty parallelism   a failure to create grammatically parallel structures when appropriate, is referred to as faulty parallelism.

figurative idiom   expressions so common that they have become clichés.

future perfect   a verb tense that indicates action in a future time in relation to another time farther in the future; it is formed with *will have* and the past participle of the verb.

future tense   a verb tense that indicates the action has yet to take place.

gerund   a noun created from the *-ing* form of a verb; gerunds act as subjects and objects in sentences.

gerund phrase   phrases that begin with the *-ing* form of a verb and have objects and modifiers; a gerund phrase always acts as a noun in a sentence, not as an adjective.

idiom   an accepted phrase or expression that doesn't follow the usual patterns of language, or has a meaning other than the literal.

imperative   refers to the mood of the verb used in requests and commands.

indefinite pronouns   (*all, any, he, she, it,* and so on) stand in for nouns but do not specify the persons or things to which they refer.

independent clause   a clause that contains a subject and a predicate, expresses a complete thought, and can stand alone as a sentence.

indicative   refers to a mood of the verb that is used in most statements and questions.

indirect object   tells to or for whom an action is done, although the words to and for are not used; it is used with a transitive verb and precedes the direct object.

indirect question   a question that is being reported rather than asked and ends with a period rather than a question mark.

infinitive   the base form of a verb with *to,* and that usually functions as a noun, although it can be an adjective or adverb.

infinitive phrase   a phrase containing an infinitive and its objects and modifiers; infinitive phrases usually function as nouns, although they can be used as adjectives and adverbs.

intensifiers   words intended to add force to what you say.

interjection   words that express a burst of emotion but are not grammatically related to other elements in a sentence.

interrogative pronoun   (*who, whom, whose, which, what*) introduce questions.

intransitive verb   verbs that do not take an object.

introduction   beginnings of essays that establish the purpose and tone; introductions should attract the reader's attention and guide the reader naturally into the rest of the paper.

irregular verb   verbs that form the past tense and past participle in a variety of ways, but not by adding *-d* or *-ed* as regular verbs do.

jargon   the specialized language of a field or profession.

linking verb   verbs that do not convey action but help complete statements about the subject by describing or identifying it.

misplaced modifier   modifiers that do not clearly relate to the word they are modifying.

modifier   describes or limits another word or group of words.

mood   refers to the manner or attitude of the speaker which the verb intends to convey; verbs have three moods: indicative, imperative, or subjunctive.

noun   a word that names a person, place, or thing, and can be either concrete or abstract.

noun clause   a clause that serves as a noun in a sentence.

number   refers to whether a noun or verb is singular or plural.

object of the preposition   a noun or pronoun that follows a preposition and completes the prepositional phrase.

objective case   when a noun or pronoun is the object of a verb, it is in the objective case.

outline   establishes an overall pattern of organization for an essay; they may be formal or informal but are essential to good writing.

paragraph   develops one idea with a series of logically connected sentences and may vary in length.

paragraph coherence   the smooth logical flow of a paragraph.

paragraph unity   a paragraph that focuses on one idea and one idea only.

parallelism   refers to matching grammatical structures; elements in a sentence that have the same function or express similar ideas should be grammatically parallel, or grammatically matched.

paraphrase   involves borrowing an idea that you rephrase in your own words.

parentheses   punctuation devices used to set off incidental information.

participle   a verb that ends in *-ing* (present participle) or *-ed, -d, -t, -en, -n* (past participle).

participial phrase   begins with a past or present participle and is followed by its object and modifiers; participial phrases are used as adjectives.

parts of speech   there are eight parts of speech: noun, verb, pronoun, adjective, adverb, preposition, conjunction, and interjection.

passive voice   see *voice.*

past perfect   a verb tense indicating action in past times in relation to another past time; it is formed with *had* and the past participle of the verb.

past tense   a verb tense indicating that an action is finished or complete.

period   punctuation device used with statements, requests, mild exclamations, courtesy questions, and abbreviations.

person   refers to the person (or thing) that is a subject or object; person can be either first (*I, me, my, mine*), second (*you, your*), or third (*he, she, him, her, it, they*).

personal pronoun   (*I, me, he, she, it,* and so on) stand in for one or more persons or things and differ in form depending upon their case.

phrase   a group of related words that have no subject-predicate combination and cannot stand alone as a sentence.

plagiarism   the use of another writer's words or ideas without acknowledging that person's contribution.

possessive case   the case of a noun or pronoun used to show ownership.

predicate   part of a sentence that tells what the subject does or is, or what is done to the subject.

preposition   shows the relationship between a noun or pronoun and another noun or pronoun.

prepositional idiom   an expression that depends on the choice of a particular preposition.

prepositional phrase   a phrase that begins with a preposition and includes a noun or pronoun that is the object of the preposition.

present perfect   a verb tense that indicates action in past time in relation to present time; it is formed with *has* or *have* and the past participle of the verb.

present tense   a verb tense that indicates the action is occurring now.

pronoun   a word that stands in for a noun.

pronoun agreement   a pronoun must agree with its antecedent in number (singular or plural) and gender (masculine or feminine).

pronoun case   refers to the way a pronoun is used in a sentence (see *objective case, possessive case, subjective [nominative] case*).

proper noun names a specific person or place, or a particular event or group and is always capitalized.

punctuation helps a reader make sense of what you write; punctuation devices include periods, question marks, exclamation points, commas, semicolons, colons, dashes, parentheses, and brackets.

question mark used to end questions.

quotation marks used to indicate to the reader that the words or sentences within the quotation marks are borrowed from another writer.

redundancy the unnecessary repetition of words, phrases, or ideas in writing.

reflexive (intensive) pronoun combines a personal pronoun with *-self* or *-selves* in order to reflect nouns or pronouns, or to provide emphasis.

relative clause a clause that begins with a relative pronoun and functions as an adjective.

relative pronoun (*who, whom, which, that*) introduce clauses that describe nouns or pronouns.

run-on sentence or comma splice is an error in which two independent clauses are joined without the proper punctuation.

semicolon punctuation device used to join independent clauses between items in a series.

sentence a group of words containing a subject and a predicate and expressing a complete thought.

sentence fragment a group of words that is missing a subject, a predicate, or does not express a complete thought.

simple predicate a verb or verb phrase.

simple sentence has one independent clause and no subordinate clauses.

simple subject a noun or pronoun.

slang conversational or informal language, which should generally be avoided in formal writing.

split infinitives breaking up an infinitive with one or more adverbs.

subject part of a sentence that tells what or whom the sentence is about.

subjective (nominative) case when a noun or pronoun is the subject of a verb.

subject-predicate agreement a predicate must agree in person and in number with its subject, regardless of other elements in a sentence.

subordinate (dependant) clause a clause that does not express a complete thought and is not a sentence; it depends upon something else to express a complete thought.

subjunctive refers to the mood of the verb used in sentences that are contrary-to-fact or hypothetical.

subordinating conjunctions join subordinate clauses to independent clauses.

superlative degree used with adjectives and adverbs to compare more than two things, people, or actions.

tense refers to the time in which the action, or state of being of the verb, is taking place.

topic the general idea or area of an essay; provides the subject of the essay.

transitive verbs a verb that takes a direct object; that is, the verb transmits action to an object.

thesis a sentence or group of sentences that make an assertion about the topic; it is usually found in the introduction and may be directly stated or implied.

verb conveys the action performed by a subject, expresses the state of that subject, or links the subject to a complement.

verb agreement see *subject-predicate agreement.*

verbal words derived from verbs but that function differently from a verb (see *gerund, infinitive, participle*).

voice refers to the form of a verb indicating whether the subject performs the action (*active voice*) or receives the action (*passive voice*).

wordy expression expressions that say the same thing twice or avoid getting directly to the point.

Appendix

FREQUENTLY CONFUSED WORDS

Some words are easy to confuse, and choosing the right word is important. Words that sound alike can be spelled differently, and words that are not acceptable usage are mistakenly used for the appropriate words. You may have to choose between words that are very similar but not interchangeable. Always check a dictionary if you are uncertain about using a word. However, you should remember that words can sometimes develop a different meaning over time. This appendix provides a valuable list of many of the commonly confused words that frustrate writers.

a, an: Use the article **a** before words that begin with consonant sounds and words that begin with a *"yew"* sound: *a bag, a plan, a historic treaty, a union, a one-armed man (one* is pronounced as if it begins with a *w).* Use **an** before words that begin with a vowel sound: *an advertisement, an hour* (the *h* is silent), *an NBC executive (NBC* sounds as if it begins with *e).*

alot, a lot: **A lot** is a colloquial expression meaning *very much* or *very many;* avoid using it in formal writing. **Alot** is a misspelling of *a lot.*

a while, awhile: These words mean essentially the same thing, but there is a distinction to be aware of. **While** means *period of time,* and therefore it is correct to write *He left for a while.* However, **awhile** means *for a period of time,* with the *for* as part of the definition. Therefore, it is correct to write *He waited awhile* but not *He waited for awhile.*

accept, except: **Accept** means *to receive* or *to agree with*: *I accept the gift; I accept your proposal.* **Except** as a preposition means *leaving out* or (as a verb) *to exclude*: *Everyone except you is invited; He was excepted from the requirement.*

adapt, adopt: When you **adapt** something, you change it to suit a purpose, such as adapting a novel for a screenplay, or adapting yourself to a new environment. When you **adopt** something, you take it as it is and make it your own. For example, the local chapter of a club may *adopt* its national organization's constitution.

adverse, averse: Adverse means *unfavorable. Adverse conditions make a trip unlikely.* **Averse** means *disinclined* or *reluctant: The secretaries are averse to changing the dress code.*

advice, advise: Advice is a noun: *Take my advice.* **Advise** is a verb: *I advise you not to go.*

affect, effect: The most common mistake here is to confuse the verb **affect** with the noun **effect**. The verb **affect** means *to influence,* while the noun **effect** means *result. The decision to strike affects us all because the effect of a strike at this time will be devastating.* (If you can put *the* in front of it, the word is *effect.*) Less frequently, **effect** is used as a verb meaning *to bring about, to accomplish: Harris effected a change in company policy.* Still less frequently, and with the accent on the first syllable, *affect* is used as a noun meaning *an emotion* or *mood as a factor in behavior* or a *stimulus arousing an emotion or mood.* The use of this noun is limited to psychology.

aid, aide: Aid means *assistance* (noun) and *to assist* (verb). It doesn't mean a person who is an assistant. That word is **aide:** *Her aide spoke to the press.*

all ready, already: All ready means all prepared. *I am all ready to go on the picnic.* **Already** means *by* or *before the given* or *implied time: I was already aware that the plan wouldn't work.*

all right, alright: All right, meaning safe, is correct; *His performance was all right.* **Alright** is an incorrect spelling.

all together, altogether: All together means *all at one time or in one place: When we rescued the five men, they were all together on the ledge.* **Altogether** means *completely, in all. Altogether, we rescued five men.*

allude, refer: To **allude** to something is to speak of it without specifically mentioning it: *When he said his father was unable to care for himself, he was probably alluding to the filthy house and empty refrigerator.* To **refer** to something is to mention it directly: *He referred to the filthy house and empty refrigerator as evidence that his father couldn't live alone.*

allusion, illusion, delusion: An *allusion* is an indirect reference: *When she spoke of Robert's listening to the ghost of his father, it was an allusion to Hamlet's behavior in Shakespeare's play.* An **illusion** is a false idea or unreal image: *The security system created the illusion that they were safe.* A **delusion** is a false belief, usually pathological: *Suffering from the delusion that he was Superman, he tried to fly.*

altar, alter: The noun **altar** is a platform used for sacred purposes, while the verb **alter** means *to change: Reverend Wolfe asked them not to alter the altar.*

alternate, alternative; alternately, alternatively: Alternate as an adjective means *every other. They meet on alternate Mondays.* **Alternative** means *providing a choice between things: The alternative plan is to meet on alternate Tuesdays.*

As adverbs, **alternately** means *one after the other*, whereas **alternatively** means *one or the other: The day was alternately sunny and stormy, He could have decided to stay home or, alternatively, to dress lightly but carry a raincoat and umbrella.*

amid, amidst: You may use either. **Amid** is more common in America, and **amidst** is more common in Britain.

among, between: In general, use **between** for two items or people and **among** for more than two items or people: *The money was to be divided between Romy and Jonathan; The money was to be divided among Romy, Jonathan, and Brian. Among* suggests a looser relationship than *between*, and therefore when three or more things are brought into a close, reciprocal relationship, such as they would be with a treaty, *between* is better than *among: The treaty between Germany, France, and Italy was never ratified,*

amount, number: Amount refers to a bulk or mass: *No amount of money would be enough.* **Number** refers to individual countable items: *He took a large number of stamps* and not *He took a large amount of stamps.*

analysis, analyzation: Always use **analysis:** *Bradford's analysis* (not **analyzation**) *of the situation is inadequate in several ways.*

any one, anyone: Use **any one** when you are referring to a particular person or thing: *Any one of the three girls is qualified.* Otherwise, use **anyone:** *Anyone can pick up a free copy.*

any way, anyway, anyways: Use **any way** as an adjective-noun pair. *I can't think of any way we can lose.* **Anyway** is an adverb meaning *in any case: Our star player was sick, but we won the game anyway.* **Anyways** is substandard and always incorrect in formal writing.

avenge, revenge: To **avenge** is to punish a wrong with the idea of seeing justice done. **Revenge** is harsher and/or less concerned with justice than with retaliating by inflicting harm: *Her father avenged her death by working to have the man arrested, tried, and convicted, while her boyfriend took revenge by killing the man's wife.*

average, mean, median: Statistically, the **average** of a group of numbers is the result of dividing their sum by the number of quantities in the group. (For example, the *average* of 3, 4, 6, and 7 is 20 divided by 4, or 5.) *Average* is also used outside statistics to mean *ordinary, typical.* The **mean** is the same as the *average.* (For example, the *mean* temperature of a day whose low is 30 degrees and whose high is 60 degrees is 45 degrees—30 plus 60 is 90 divided by 2 equals 45.) The **median** is the point in a series of ascending or descending numbers where half the numbers in the series are on one side and half on the other. (For example, in the series 5, 7, 9, 12, and 16, the *median* is 9.)

beside, besides: Beside means *next to, at the side of,* **besides** means *in addition to*: *Besides, I don't want to spend my life beside the dump.*

biannual, biennial: Biannual means twice a year, **biennial** means *every two years.*

bimonthly, biweekly: Bimonthly can mean either *every two months* or *twice a month.* **Biweekly** can mean either *every two weeks* or *twice a week.* Because of these dual meanings, it is clearer to use terms such as *twice a month* and *every two months* instead.

bloc, block: Use **block** except when referring to a coalition of people or nations. Then the word is **bloc:** *The gun-control bloc* (not *block*) *defeated the amendment.*

can, may: Can means *having the power to do something* and **may** means *having permission to do it.* However, current usage allows the use of both to indicate permission: *The president says Mr. Downie can speak at the meeting, The president says Mr. Downie may speak at the meeting.* May is more formal, but can is not wrong.

capital, capitol: Use **capital** when referring to the city that is the seat of a government; use **capitol** when referring to the building where a legislature meets: *The capital of California is Sacramento. When we arrived there, we toured the capitol and other government buildings.*

censor, censure: To **censor** something is to edit, remove, or prohibit it because it is judged objectionable; to **censure** someone is to strongly condemn him or her as wrong: *The vice principal censured the class president for her fiery speech, but he didn't censor the speech.*

cite, site, sight: Cite is a verb meaning *to summon before a court of law, to mention by way of example, or to officially mention as meritorious: I am citing you for creating a public nuisance; I cited the first chapter of the book as* *proof of my argument; The young officer was cited for bravery.* **Site** is a noun meaning *location or scene: We drove quickly to the site of the murder.* **Sight** is also a noun, meaning *the ability to see or something seen. From the hill, the stormy ocean was a beautiful sight.*

compare with, compare to; contrast with, contrast to: To compare things means to cite their similarities, differences, or both. **To contrast** means to cite differences.

Use **compare to** when stating a likeness between things: *The final scene in the novel can be compared to the final scene in the play, since both show a rec- onciliation of opposing forces.* Use **compare with** when showing similarities, differences, or both: *Compared with what was budgeted for prisons, the amount budgeted for crime prevention was small, but both amounts were up from last year's.*

Use **contrast to** when showing things with opposite characteristics: *The Smiths' peaceful marriage is in contrast to the Nelsons' bitter relationship.* Use **contrast with** when juxtaposing things to illustrate their differences: *They contrasted Mr. Headley's plan for bringing in new businesses with Ms. Friedman's.*

complement, compliment: As a noun, **complement** means *something which completes or perfects something else, and, as a verb, to accompany or complete something else: His creativity was the perfect complement to her deter- mination, The wine complemented the main course.* **Compliment** as a noun means *something said in praise, and as a verb to praise: Her compliment about his dancing pleased him, he in turn complimented her on her gracefulness.*

compose, comprise: **Compose** means *to make up. Two senators from each state compose the U.S. Senate.* **Comprise** means *to include: The U.S. Senate comprises two senators from each state.* The most common mistake is to use *comprise* for *compose. Remember that the whole comprises the parts, not the other way around.* Also, don't use the phrase *is comprised of.*

conscience, consciousness: **Conscience** is an inner voice, a sense of right and wrong, whereas **consciousness** is simply awareness, or the ability to think and feel: *Consciousness of the old woman's plight didn't seem to bother his conscience.* The adjectival forms are **conscientious**, which means *scrupu- lous, painstaking, or acting in accordance with conscience,* and **conscious,** which means *awake or aware.*

contemptible, contemptuous: **Contemptible** means *deserving contempt,* while **contemptuous** means *showing or feeling contempt: We were con- temptuous of their feeble explanation for their contemptible behavior toward the animals.*

continual, continuous: Something that is **continual** *is* repeated often. Something that is **continuous** goes on without interruption: *I made continual requests for a seat change because of the baby's continuous crying.*

council, counsel: Council, a noun, is a committee or an administrative body. **Counsel** as a noun is *advice, an exchange of ideas, or a lawyer or group of lawyers: Her counsel advised her that she should first seek counsel from an expert and then approach the town council. Council* is never a verb. *Counsel* as a verb means *to give advice. She counseled him to increase his investments in the stock market.*

denote, connote: Denote refers to the dictionary definition of a word: *The noun "rose" denotes a particular flower.* **Connote** means what a word may imply or suggest. For example, the noun *rose* can *connote* youth, beauty, the impermanence of beauty, freshness, etc. *Connotations* include all the suggestions and overtones that are beyond a word's dictionary definition.

device, devise: A device (noun) is an instrument, either something concrete like a can opener or something abstract like a plan. **Devise,** a verb, means *to create or fashion a device: They devised an ingenious device for pitting olives.*

different from, different than: When comparing two things, use **different from:** *The movie is different from* (not *than*) *the book, My goals are different from* (not *than*) *yours.* If **different** introduces a subordinate clause, use the subordinating conjunction **than:** *The true story was different than I had believed.*

dilemma, problem: Don't use **dilemma** carelessly to mean **problem**. A **dilemma** means *a choice between two unattractive alternatives: Her dilemma was whether to put up with her neighbor's noise or to give up the inexpensive apartment.* A **problem** doesn't necessarily involve such a choice: *The problem of how to provide universal health care plagued us,* not *The dilemma of how to provide universal health care plagued us.*

discreet, discrete: If you are **discreet** you are careful about what you do and say; you show prudence and good judgment. **Discrete,** however, means *separate and distinct. It was discreet of the maid to divide the laundry into discrete piles, one of Bob's clothes and one of Tony's.*

disinterested, uninterested: Disinterested means *impartial,* and **uninterested** means *lacking interest.* A jury that is *disinterested* is desirable; a jury that is *uninterested* is not, because the members may doze off during the trial.

dual, duel: Dual is an adjective meaning *double* or *twofold*, while **duel** is a noun meaning *a fight* or *contest*.

e.g., i.e: The abbreviation **e.g.** (from the Latin *exempli gratia*) means *for example*. Do not confuse it with the abbreviation i.e. (from the Latin *id est*), which means *that is (to say)*. Use *e.g.* (which should be preceded and followed by commas) when you are citing some but not all examples: *He took many camping items with him, e.g., a tent, a cooking stove, a lantern, and a sleeping bag.* Do not use *etc.* with *e.g.* because the idea of more examples than are being cited is already present in *e.g.* Use **i.e.,** also enclosed in commas, when you are presenting an equivalent of the preceding term: *He will study the document, i.e., the committee's official confirmation.* In a formal essay you should write out *for example* and *that is* rather than using the abbreviations.

emigrate, immigrate: When you leave a country, you **emigrate** from it. When you come into a country, you **immigrate** to it: *His parents, who emigrated from Russia, immigrated to the United States.*

eminent, imminent, emanate: Eminent means *prominent*, while **imminent** means *about to happen*: *The eminent lawyer was in imminent danger of being shot.* **Emanate** means *to issue from a source: A ghostly light emanated from the cloud.*

entitled, titled: Use **entitled** to mean *the right to have or do something: The Doyles were entitled to the money.* Do not use it to mean **titled.** *The book is titled* (not *entitled*) *The Habitats of Wolves.*

envelop, envelope: Envelop is a verb meaning *to cover completely* or *surround: The fog envelops the town.* **Envelope** is a noun meaning *something that covers,* such as an *envelope* for a letter.

envy, jealousy: Although sometimes used synonymously, *envy* and *jealousy* have different meanings. **Envy** is the desire for something that someone else has, or a feeling of ill will over another's advantages in general: *My envy of your success has made me bitter.* **Jealousy** is a resentful suspicion that someone else has what rightfully belongs to the jealous person: *Out of jealousy, he followed his wife; The favored treatment of the daughter created jealousy in the son.*

et al., etc.,: The abbreviation **et al.** (Latin *et alit*) means *and others.* It, rather than *etc.,* should be used to refer to additional people: *The research paper was prepared by S. Robinson, F Lupu, I Alderson, et al.* Use this abbreviation only in informal writing and in bibliographical entries or similar citations. The abbreviation **etc.** (Latin *et cetera*) also means *and others,* but it is used with things, not people: *Don't forget to collect test papers, pencils,* *scratch pads, etc.* Although *etcetera* or *etc.* is acceptable in instructional texts with many examples or in informal reports, use *and so forth* in the text of a formal essay. If you use the phrase *such as* before a list of items, don't use *etc.*: *Gym equipment, such as basketballs, nets, and towels, will be provided* not *Gym equipment, such as basketballs, nets, towels, etc., will be provided.*

every one, everyone: Every one means *each one of a group of particular items or people: Every one of those people who came to the party early left drunk.* **Everyone** means *all, everybody: Everyone left the party drunk.*

farther, further: Use **farther** in referring to physical distance: *I walked farther than you.* Otherwise, use **further:** *I will question the suspect further; She went further with her claims.*

faze, phase: Faze is a verb meaning *to disturb or daunt,* **phase** is a noun meaning *a period or stage: This phase of her son's behavior didn't faze her.* As a verb, **phase** (with in) means *to introduce or carry out in stages: They phased in the new equipment at the plant.*

fewer, less: Use **fewer** for individual countable items or people; use **less** for bulk or quantity: *We expected fewer (not less) people to come; They stole less (not fewer) than twenty dollars.* (Here, *twenty dollars* is a single quantity, a lump sum.)

flair, flare: If you have a **flair** for something, you have a natural talent for it: *Her flair for putting people at ease impressed us.* A **flare** is a flame or bright light. **Flare** as verb means *to blaze brightly or burst out suddenly.* **Flair** is never a verb.

flaunt, flout: Flaunt means *to make a gaudy or defiant display of something.* It is sometimes confused with **flout,** which means *to scorn or mock: He flouted (not flaunted) convention by wearing jeans to the black-tie dinner; She flaunted (not flouted) her company car in front of the clerks.*

forward, foreword: Forward means *ahead,* or *at or toward the front.* Don't use it when you mean **foreword,** an introductory statement at the beginning of a book.

fortunate, fortuitous: Fortunate means *lucky, having good fortune. Fortuitous* means *happening by chance.* A **fortuitous** event isn't necessarily favorable: *It was merely fortuitous that she was standing at the cliff's edge when the landslide began, but she was fortunate enough to escape death.*

fulsome, abundant: Don't use *fulsome* when you mean **abundant** (*profuse* or *great quantity*). **Fulsome** means *excessive or offensive.* Therefore, receiving *fulsome* praise for an action is not something to be happy about, while receiving *abundant* praise is.

gamut, gauntlet: Gamut means *the entire range or extent: His reactions ran the gamut from rage to apathy.* Don't confuse this word with *gauntlet.* **Gauntlet** has two meanings. First, it refers to a glove which in the days of chivalry was thrown to the ground to announce a challenge. Therefore, *throwing down the gauntlet* has become a figure of speech meaning to challenge: *A fifty-year-old woman entered the race, thus throwing down the gauntlet before the younger runners.* Second, **gauntlet** was also once a form of punishment in which a person ran between two rows of men who struck him. It has also become a figure of speech: *In trying to promote her idea, she was forced to run the gauntlet between those who thought it was too ambitious and those who thought it wasn't ambitious enough.*

grisly, grizzly: A crime is **grisly** (that is, ghastly, terrifying). A bear, or someone whose hair is partially gray, is **grizzly:** *Meeting a grizzly bear in the woods could be a grisly experience.*

hanged, hung: Although the usual past and past participle of hang is **hung, hanged** is still preferred when referring to people: *We hung the paintings yesterday* BUT *We hanged the murderer last week.*

historic, historical: If something is **historic,** it *figures in* history. If something is **historical,** it *pertains to* history. Betsy Ross's home is a *historic* building, the Alamo is a *historic* site, the moon landing is a *historic* event. On the other hand, you may take a *historical* tour of Washington, read a *historical* novel by Irving Stone, or buy a book of *historical* maps.

ignorant, stupid: Don't use *stupid* when you mean *ignorant.* If you are **ignorant** of something, you simply don't know it: *I was ignorant of the plans to rebuild the area when I suggested we make some repairs.* If you are **stupid,** you are lacking normal intelligence: *Because he was considered stupid, he was not allowed to join the corps.*

implicit, tacit, explicit: Implicit means *implied or unstated;* however, it can also mean *without reservation,* which sometimes causes confusion. In a statement such as *The consequences of the action were implicit in the letter,* it is obvious that the meaning is implied. But the meaning is ambiguous in a statement such as *Their trust in the committee was implicit.* Does *implicit* mean the trust was implied rather than stated, or does it mean the trust was beyond question? It would be better to say either *Their trust in the committee was left implicit* (that is, unstated) or *Their trust in the committee was absolute.* **Tacit** means *unspoken,* not *expressed openly,* and is therefore similar to one of the meanings of *implicit.* *Tacit,* however, is used in reference to speech rather than general expression: *Although he didn't specifically address her, his speech gave her the tacit approval she needed to continue* *her project.* **Explicit** is the opposite of implicit, means clearly stated: *The professor was explicit in presenting the course requirements.*

imply, infer: Imply means *to suggest something indirectly.* **Infer** means *to conclude from facts or indications.* If I *imply* by yawning that I'm tired, you might *infer* that I want you to leave. Think of *implying* as done by the actor, *inferring* as done by the receiver.

The most common error is to use infer when imply is correct: *To influence the buyer, the owner implied* (not *inferred*) *that the property would increase in value within a few months; All the reports implied* (not *inferred*) *that the death was a suicide.*

incredible, incredulous: Incredible means unbelievable or so astonishing as to seem unbelievable, whereas **incredulous** means skeptical or unbelieving: We were incredulous as we listened to his incredible story about being abducted by aliens. Avoid the colloquial (and imprecise) use of incredible to mean striking or very, as in That's an incredible dress you're wearing, or I was incredibly sad.

inflammable, flammable: Inflammable and **flammable** both mean *easily set on fire, will burn readily.* Because people might think *inflammable* means *not easily set on fire* (as *inactive* means *not active, incoherent* means *not coherent,* etc.), those who deal with fires and fire insurance argue that flammable should be used for warning signs and labels.

irregardless, regardless: The use of **irregardless** has become an epidemic, but it is not an acceptable word. The word is always **regardless**: *Regardless of what you think, the changes will be made.* With people who know language, *irregardless* is a glaring error.

its, it's: Its is the possessive of *it: The tree lost its leaves.* **It's** is a contraction meaning *it is: It's too bad we can't come.*

lay, lie: These verbs cause trouble for many people. If you mean *repose,* use **lie.** If you mean *set* or *put,* use **lay.** An easy way to remember which one to use is to recognize that *lie* does not take an object and *lay* does: *I lie down for a nap everyday, The dog lies by the fire; I lay the paper on the table, I lay myself down* (here *myself* becomes the object). The past tense and the past participles of lie are lay and lain: *I lay down for a nap yesterday, I have lain down every afternoon this week.* The past and past participle of *lay* are *laid* and *laid: I laid the paper on the table yesterday; I have laid it in the same spot for years.*

lead, led (verbs): **Led** is the past tense of **lead:** *Last week he led the march; I usually lead it, but I was ill.*

libel, slander: Legally, **slander** means *to defame someone orally, as in a speech or public remark.* **Libel** is to defame someone by any other means, such as in print, pictures, films, or signs.

like, as: Both **as** and **like** can be used as prepositions: *He sleeps like a baby; We see this as an alternative.* But only as is a subordinating conjunction, so when you are introducing a clause, don't use *like: The storm started after lunch, just as* (not *like) I said it would, He smiled as* (not *like) his brother used to when I gave advice.*

lightning, lightening: **Lightning** is a flash of light. **Lightening** means *getting lighter.*

limp, limpid: Don't use limpid as a synonym for limp. **Limpid** means *crystal clear,* not wilted or lacking in stiffness or backbone (**limp**): *Instead of the limp* (not *limpid), frail young girl who had come to our door, we were now faced with a strong, self-confident woman with a steady, limpid gaze.*

literally, figuratively: **Literally** means *true to the meaning of the words,* or *precisely as stated.* It is often misused to mean *almost* or *definitely,* as in *I literally died when he chose me.* If you literally died, you would be talking from beyond the grave. In the sentence *I literally died when he chose me, died* is being used not literally but **figuratively,** that is, as a metaphor for the overwhelming reaction you experienced. To convey your emotion metaphorically, you could say, *I almost died when he chose me.* Use *literally* only when referring to the meaning precisely as stated: *By blocking the door, he literally refused to let anyone leave the room; The literal subject of the poem is the flowers, but the poet is using them figuratively to represent the impermanence of beauty.*

loath, loathe: **Loath** is an adjective meaning *reluctant.* **Loathe** is a verb meaning *to despise. I am loath to admit that I loathe David.*

lose, loose: **Lose** means *to be unable to find.* **Loose,** an adjective, means *unrestrained or inexact: I lose the loose change I keep in my pocket; The poem loses its power in such a loose translation.* Loose is used less frequently as a verb. It *means to set free or make less tight. She loosed the snake into the crowd; He loosed* (more commonly, *loosened) the victim's clothing.*

nauseous, nauseated: When you're sick to your stomach, you're **nauseated.** The thing that made you sick—for example, rotten meat— is **nauseous.** Twirling the baby and throwing him up in the air makes him *nauseated* (not *nauseous).* The baby would be *nauseous* only if the sight of him made someone else feel *nauseated.*

noisome, noisy: *Noisome* is not a fancy version of **noisy**. **Noisome** means *harmful* or *offensive*, especially related to smell.

oral, verbal, written: Oral means *uttered, spoken.* **Verbal** means *of, in,* or *by means of words,* whether the words are spoken or written. An *oral* agreement is an unwritten agreement. A *verbal agree*ment can be either a spoken or written agreement. To avoid confusion, use *oral* or *written* instead of the ambiguous *verbal.* Reserve *verbal* for situations in which you are distinguishing communication in words from other types of communication, such as sign language and body movements.

passed, past: Passed is a verb: *I passed the test; We passed the old barn on our way here.* **Past** is either a noun, an adjective, or a preposition—but never a verb: *The past haunts us; His past sins caught up with him; The lake lies past the barn.*

precede, proceed: Precede means *to go before in time, place, rank,* etc.: *His remarks preceded the musical program.* **Proceed** means *to move forward*: *Before we proceed, we should be sure of the rules.* Since the meaning of proceed includes the idea of moving forward, don't use it as a fancy word for *go,* particularly in situations when the movement isn't forward: *They went back (or returned) to the car* not *They proceeded back to the car.*

predominant, predominate: Predominant is an adjective meaning *having authority or influence over others, being superior,* or *being most frequent: The predominant group at the convention was opposed to his candidacy, and therefore he lost. The predominant reason they gave for their opposition was his moral character.* **Predominate** is a verb meaning *to be dominant. Noise and confusion predominated at the convention.*

preventive, preventative: Preventive and **preventative** mean the same thing—something that prevents—but choose *preventive: Our goal is to take preventive measures so that a riot after the game will be unlikely.*

principal, principle: Principal as an adjective means *first in importance.* As a noun, **principal** means *the head of a school. The principal reason that Nelson was chosen to be principal of our school was her dedication.* **Principle** is a noun meaning *a fundamental truth or law upon which others are based, or a rule of conduct: The principal's principles were questioned by the parent group.*

prone, supine: If you are **prone,** you are lying face downward. If you are **supine,** you are lying face upward.

prostate, prostrate: The **prostate** is a male gland. **Prostrate,** an adjective, means *lying prone* or *overcome.* The common misuse is *prostrate* for *prostate: He has recovered from prostate cancer* BUT *She was prostrate from the heat.*

ravage, ravish: **Ravage** means *to destroy violently or to devastate,* while **ravish** means *to abduct, to rape, or to transport with joy or delight: The troops ravaged* (not *ravished*) *all the cities they entered; The villain ravished* (not *ravaged*) *the beautiful maiden; The soprano's voice ravished* (not *ravaged*) *his ears and left him with a beatific smile.*

rebut, refute: The common error is to use *refute* for *rebut.* When you **rebut** an opponent's argument, you speak or write against it. When you **refute** an argument, you actually disprove it. Whether you have *refuted* your opponent's argument is often a matter of opinion. Avoid using it loosely: *The government spokesperson rebutted* (not *refuted*) *the argument that the war on drugs had been a disaster.*

recur, reoccur: **Recur** and **reoccur** mean the same thing—*to happen again.* But careful writers make a fine distinction. *Reoccur* is used to mean *to happen one more time,* while *recur* indicates *a repetition more than once,* usually *according to a schedule or pattern: Her terror reoccurred when she saw her attacker in the courtroom,* but *The recurring movement of the tides changed the shoreline.*

regretfully, regrettably: **Regretfully** means *filled with regret.* Don't use it in place of **regrettably,** which means *in a manner that calls for regret. Regrettably* (not *regretfully*), *the militia was too late to save the small village. The soldiers watched regretfully as the buildings burned.*

reticent, reluctant: Don't use reticent as a synonym for reluctant. **Reticent** means *disinclined to speak,* not just *disinclined or unwilling* (**reluctant**): *The group was reticent about its reluctance to admit new members.*

shall, will: *Will* has generally replaced *shall* in modern usage. In the future tense *I* and *we* can be accompanied by **shall** rather than *will,* but **will** is more common. **Shall** is also sometimes used to indicate a commanding tone (*You shall eat everything on your plate*), or determination (*We shall overcome*). *Will* is acceptable in these cases; *shall* creates a more formal effect.

sit, set: **Sit** usually doesn't take an object: *I sit down.* **Set** usually does: *I set the book down.* Don't use them interchangeably: *Set* (not *Sit*) *that load down and sit* (not *set*) *down and talk to me.* **Sit** can take an object when it means *to cause to sit, to seat: I sat Grandpa in the easy chair and called the doctor.* **Set** doesn't take an object when it means *to sit on eggs; to become firm (Let the cement set overnight); to begin to move (We set forth yesterday);* or *to sink below the horizon (The sun sets).*

some time, sometime, sometimes: Some time is a span of time: *Some time passed before she came in.* **Sometime** means *at an unspecified time: We should get together sometime.* **Sometimes** means *at times: Sometimes I'm so nervous I can't sleep.*

stationary, stationery: Confusion of these two words is a spelling problem: **Stationary** means *still, at rest;* **stationery** is paper.

tack, tact: One meaning of the noun **tack** is *a course of action or policy, especially one differing from a preceding course,* as in the sentence *He decided to take a different tack.* A common mistake is to use the noun *tact* in such contexts. **Tact** means, among other things, *sensitive skill in dealing with people,* or *diplomacy.*

than, then: Don't use **then** (which means *at that time*) in comparisons. Use **than**: *He is wiser than* (not *then*) *his father was then.*

their, there, they're: Their is the possessive form of *they;* **there** usually refers to place or is used in impersonal constructions *(there is, there are);* **they're** is a contraction of *they are.* Notice the correct uses of these words in the following sentence: *There is no question that their friends live there and that they're willing to help.*

themselves, theirselves: Themselves, which is an emphatic form of them, is correct, as in, *The authors themselves left the theater;* **theirselves** is not acceptable usage.

thus, thusly: Use **thus**, meaning *in this way,* not **thusly;** as in, *Thus, it came to pass.*

to, too: To *has several meanings, the first being toward.* **Too** *means also or more than enough: I walked to the river, which was too wild for me to swim in. My father thought so too.*

tortuous, torturous: Tortuous means *full of twists and turns: a tortuous mountain road, a tortuous plot.* **Torturous** means *severely painful, agonizing. The trek across the Sahara was torturous.*

toward, towards: You may use either, but **toward** is used more frequently in America, while **towards** is used more often in Britain.

usage, use, utilize: Usage means *established practice.* Don't use it as a substitute for the noun **use**: *Use* (not *Usage*) *of gloves is recommended.* A more common tendency is to replace the verb *use* with **utilize** and the noun *use* with **utilization**, but this is not recommended. Prefer *use: We want to use* (not *utilize*) *our assets wisely, Use* (not *Utilization*) *of out-of-date equipment has become a major problem.*

waive, wave: The correct expression is *to waive one's rights* not *to wave one's rights*. **Waive** means *to relinquish*; **wave** means *move to and fro*.

weather, whether: **Weather** *is* the state of the atmosphere, while **whether** means *if*.

whose, who's: **Whose** is the possessive of who. **Who's** is a contraction of who is: *Who's going to tell me whose jacket this is?*

your, you're: **Your** is the possessive of *you*. **You're** is a contraction of *you are: You're certain this is your jacket?*

Index